SNAPSHOTS OF THE NEW TESTAMENT

I0459297

A CONCISE SUMMARY OF EVERY BOOK IN THE NEW TESTAMENT

LEE J. SMITH

Snapshots of the New Testament A Concise Summary of Every Book in the New Testament Copyrights ©2025 by Lee J. Smith

eBook ISBN: 979-8-9929284-4-0

Paperback ISBN: 979-8-9929284-3-3

Hardcover ISBN: 979-8-9929284-5-7

Copyright Registration Number: TXu 2-479-581

All Scripture quotations are from the English Standard Version, (Crossway 2001)

Table of Contents

Introduction 1

A Snapshot of the New Testament 3

A Snapshot of the Gospels 17

A Snapshot of Matthew 37

A Snapshot of Luke 56

A Snapshot of John 64

A Snapshot of Acts 73

A Snapshot of Romans 82

A Snapshot of 1 Corinthians 92

A Snapshot of 2 Corinthians 104

A Snapshot of Galatians 111

A Snapshot of Ephesians 118

A Snapshot of Philippians 126

A Snapshot of Colossians 133

A Snapshot of 1 Thessalonians 139

A Snapshot of 2 Thessalonians 145

A Snapshot of Timothy 151

A Snapshot of 1 Timothy 157

A Snapshot of 2 Timothy 164

A Snapshot of Titus 171

A Snapshot of Philemon 180

A Snapshot of Hebrews 184

A Snapshot of James 191

A Snapshot of 1 Peter 198

A Snapshot of 2 Peter 204

A Snapshot of 1 John 211

A Snapshot of 2 John 219

A Snapshot of 3 John 223

A Snapshot of Jude 228

A Snapshot of Revelation 234

Recommended Resources 241

INTRODUCTION

My purpose in writing this little survey is to give students of the Bible a resource for understanding the historical context, basic argument and practical value of each book of the New Testament of the Bible. I want the reader to have assurance that each book in the Bible has significance for understanding God's eternal plan and has value for personal spiritual development. I am totally convinced that 2 Timothy 3:16-17 speaks the truth: "All Scripture is breathed out by God and profitable for teaching, for reproof, for correction, and for training in righteousness, that the person of God may be complete, equipped for every good work."

This will not be a detailed study or a commentary. I do not intend to enter into academic debates about authorship, dates of composition, or the historical development of the books. Neither do I intend to prove the conclusions to which I have come.

This is intended to be a quick guide for non-theologically trained people who just want a better understanding of the basic content and practical application of each of the books of the Bible.

I write from an evangelical perspective, believing that the books of the Bible are God's inspired, inerrant word, which give us all we need to know to know God, gain eternal life, grow in Christlikeness, and do his will.

Some of the outlines are not original to me. Some are developed from professors at Dallas Theological Seminary. I noted the sources when I adopted an outline.

Neither you nor I will agree with everything in the recommended resources listed. I have placed an asterisk before the commentaries, which I would consider first buys.

A SNAPSHOT OF THE NEW TESTAMENT

1. The New Testament canon.

We have 27 books in our English Bible New Testament.. We have accepted these 27 books because they bear the stamp of divine authority within themselves and were thus recognized by the early church. The following evidence points to the inspiration of the New Testament books:

1) The promises of Jesus to his Apostles. John 16:13, 14:25-26.

2) The testimony (claims) of the authors. 1 Corinthians 12:13, 14:37, 1 Timothy 5:18, 1 Thessalonians 5:27, Colossians 4:16, 2 Peter 3:16 Revelation 1:1, 3, 22:18-19.

3) The great early church councils gave recognition to these books as the ones possessing God's authority.

2. The Language of the New Testament. The New Testament was originally Written in Koine Greek (the Greek used by ordinary people and not Classical literary Greek). Some believe parts of the Gospels might have been first written in Aramaic.

3. The Divisions of the New Testament

1) The Gospels. The story of Jesus Christ: his birth, miracles, teaching, death and resurrection. Matthew, Mark, Luke, and John

2) The Acts. The story of the beginning of the Church.

3) The Epistles. Letters for the churches.

(l) Written by Paul

    a. Doctrinal-Galatians, 1 & 2 Thessalonians, 1 &

        2 Corinthians, and Romans.

    b. Prison-written when Paul was in prison in

        Rome.   Ephesians,   Colossians,   and Philippians

    c. Personal-written to individuals. Philemon, 1

Timothy, Titus and 2 Timothy.

(2) Written by others: Hebrews, James 1 & 2 Peter, 1, 2, 3 John, Jude

4) Revelation-the New Testament book of prophecy.

4. Chronological Order of the New Testament

Reign of Caesar Augustus 27 b.c. –AD 14

The birth of Jesus 4 b.c

Death of Herod the Great 4 b.c. Matthew 2

Pilate procurator of Judea AD 26-36

Baptism of Jesus AD 26 Matthew 3

Death/resurrection of Jesus AD 30 Matthew 27-28

Birth of the Church AD 30 Acts 2

Conversion of Saul AD 31-33 Acts 9

Death of James AD 44 Acts 12

Epistle of James AD 44-49

Paul's 1st missionary journey AD 46-47 Acts 13-14

Epistle of Galatians AD 48

Jerusalem Council AD49-50 Acts 15:1-35

Paul's 2nd missionary journey AD 49-50

    Acts 15:36-18:21

Epistles to the Thessalonians AD 50-51

    Acts 18:1-18

Paul's 3rd missionary journey AD 52-55

    Acts 18:22-21:16

Epistles to the Corinthians AD 55-56 Acts 19-20

Epistle to the Romans AD 56-57 Acts 19

Paul's arrest in Jerusalem 57 Acts 21:16-23

Felix as procurator of Judea AD 52-59

    Acts 23:26-24:27

Paul imprisoned in Caesarea AD 57-59 Acts 24

Festus as procurator of Judea AD 59-61

    Acts 24:27-36:32

Paul's hearings AD 59   Acts 25-26

Paul's journey to Rome AD 59-60 Acts 27:1-

    28:16

Paul in prison in Rome AD 60-62 Acts 28

Gospel of Mark early AD 60s

Gospel of Matthew in the AD 60s

Epistle to the Ephesians AD 60-61

Epistle to Colossians AD 60-61

Letter to Philemon AD 60-61

Epistle to the Philippians AD 62

Gospel of Luke early AD 60s

Book of Acts AD 63

Paul's release from prison AD 62-66

1st letter to Timothy 6AD 4-66

Letter to Titus AD 64-66

Book of 1 Peter AD 62-65

Book of 2 Peter AD 66-67

2nd letter to Timothy AD 687

Epistle to the Hebrews late AD 60s

Epistle of Jude late AD 60s/early 70s

Destruction of Jerusalem AD70

Epistles of 1, 2, 3 John AD 85-90

Gospel of John AD 80s to 90s

Revelation AD 90-95

5. Historical Context of the New Testament

1) The Political Background

   (1) The Greek Period. 301 b.c. to 63 b.c.

The Persian Empire was destroyed by Alexander the Great. 331 b.c.

At Alexander's death the Greek empire split between his four generals. Palestine was under the sway of the Ptolemy regime in Egypt, then the Seleucid Regime centered in Syria.

a.   Ptolemaic Period 301 b.c. to 198 b.c. The Jews were generally well-treated and quasi-independent.

b.   Seleucid Period 198 b.c. to 63e. b.c. Jews generally ill-treated, especially by Antiochus Epiphanies (175-164 b.c.) who outlawed Sabbath observance, temple sacrifice and circumcision. He built an Altar to Zeus in the temple and sacrificed swine on it. This led to the Jewish revolt under the Maccabees.

c.   Maccabean Period 167-63b.c. The Jews Judas Maccabaeus (166-161), Jonathan Maccabaeus (161-143) and Simon Maccabaeus (143135) ruled.

(2) The Roman Period. 63 b.c. Palestine came under Roman rule under the campaign of the

Roman general Pompey in 63 b.c. Other significant dates:

49 b.c. Julius Caesar became emperor.

47 b.c. Antipater, a man of Jewish and Idumean descent was appointed procurator of Judea.

37-4 b.c. Herod the Great was the political force in Palestine.

2) The Social and Cultural Background

(1) The People. The Jews were simple, religious, non-artisans, non-political.

The Greeks, sophisticated, proud of intellectual and artistic achievements, poets, philosophers, pagans.

The Romans-practical, orderly society, politically powerful.

(2) The Languages. Latin was the language of law and government. Greek was the language of the common people and literature. Aramaic was the main language of the east including Palestine. Hebrew was the language of the rabbis but not understood by the ordinary Jew.

(3) Economics. Most people were poor, worse off than slaves. Land and wealth were in the hands of a few-the political and religious leaders. 30 to 50% of world population were slaves. Almost no middle class.

3) Religious background.

(1) Judaism-Synagogue worship. Temple rituals. Corrupt leadership. High priesthood was possessed by political appointment, bribery and intrigue. Pharisees - conservatives, largest sect, popular with people. Sadducees - liberals, powerful, corrupt, unpopular. Essenes - small bands of separatists. Zealots-fanatical nationalists, violent, rebels against Rome.

(2) Greek. The old Greek religions had faded except for in certain places like Ephesus. Local gods and nature deities. Philosophers: Epicures, Plato, Socrates, the Stoics and Cynics.

(3) Roman. Old Roman religions were dying (animistic) and emperor worship was growing,

especially toward the end of the first century A.D. General moral decay.

6. Major Themes of the New Testament

1) The Kingdom: The rule of God over his people. In the New Testament the kingdom can refer to: (1) the future rule of Christ on earth, the inner rule of Christ in one's heart or the universal rule of God over the universe.

2) Salvation through the atoning death and resurrection of Jesus Christ. Salvation includes: ast deliverance from the penalty of sin-justification,

present deliverance from the power of sin-sanctification and future deliverance from the presence of sin-glorification.

3) The Church. The Gospels are the basis for the Church. Acts records the founding of the Church. The Epistles are teaching for the Church. Revelation is the future of the Church and God's kingdom.

7. The Story of the New Testament

There are 400 years between the writing of Malachi and the first events of the New Testament. The last prophecy of Malachi was of the coming of Elijah which Jesus said referred to John the Baptist.

The Gospels tell the story of Jesus Christ. They tell of his virgin conception, his ministry of teaching, choosing the Apostles, his miracles, his atoning death, and his resurrection. He came as Israel's Messiah and the Savior whose death would save people from their sins. Each Gospel emphasizes a different aspect of his person and work. Matthew presents him as the King. Mark presents him as God's Servant. Luke shows his perfect humanity and messiahship. John presents him as God incarnate, the one sent from the Father to bring eternal life to all who will believe in him. In the Gospels, the king was rejected and the kingdom was postponed. The Savior died and was raised to life.

The book of Acts unfolds God's new program, the gathering of believers into his Church by the taking of the Gospel to the whole world. In Acts 1-12 Peter and others take the Gospel first to the Jews, then to the Samaritans and finally to the first Gentile, Cornelius. In Chapters 13-28 the Gospel spreads to the very heart of the Gentile world, Rome, by the preaching of Paul and his associates. Acts is the story of the founding of the church.

The Epistles are letters of instruction for the Church. Paul penned 13 of the epistles. They can be chronologically divided into three groups: His preaching or doctrinal epistles: Galatians, 1&2 Thessalonians, Romans, and 1&2 Corinthians; his prison epistles: Ephesians, Colossians and Philippians; and his personal epistles: Philemon, 1 & 2 Timothy and Titus. In the doctrinal epistles he establishes the Gospel. In the prison epistles he establishes Christlike living. In the personal epistles he establishes patterns of conduct of churches.

The other general epistles, not written by Paul are: Hebrews, James, 1 & 2 Peter, 1&2&3 John and Jude.

Revelation is the New Testament book of prophecy. It ties everything together. The world is judged in the great judgments of the Tribulation. Jesus Christ returns to set up the Millennial Kingdom. After the Millennium the wicked are judged and cast into The Lake of Fire. Believers who have been raised to life are placed into a new earth and dwell eternally in The New Jerusalem. Jesus Christ reigns forever. The Savior becomes the Eternal King. The promises made to Abraham (Genesis 12-15) and David (2 Samuel 7) and Israel (Jeremiah 31) are fulfilled.

Recommended Resources

Manfred T. Brauch, Hard Sayings of Paul, IVP, 1989

F.F. Bruce, New Testament History, Doubleday, 1972

F. F. Bruce, The Hard Sayings of Jesus, IVP, 1983

D. A. Carson and G. K. Beale, Commentary on the New Testament Use of the Old Testament, Baker, 2007

*D.A. Carson, Douglas Moo, and Leon Morris, An Introduction to the New Testament, Apollos IVP, 1992

Peter H, Davids, More Hard Sayings of the New Testament, IVP, 1991

Walter Elwell and Robert Yarbrough, Encountering the New Testament, Baker, 2013

R. T. France, Jesus and the Old Testament, Tyndale, 1977

Harold Hoehner, Chronological Aspects of the Life of Christ, Zondervan, 1978

James Jeffers, The Greco-Roman World of the New Testament Era, IVP, 1999

Wayne A. Meeks, The First Urban Christians, Yale, 1983

A. N. Sherwin-White, Roman Society and Roman Law in the NT, Baker, 1963

Merrill C. Tenney, New Testament Times, Eerdmans, 1965

John Walvoord and Roy Zuck, The Bible Knowledge Commentary New Testament, Cook, 1984

Roy Zook and Darrell Bock, editors, A Biblical Theology of the New Testament, Moody, 1984

A SNAPSHOT OF THE GOSPELS

1. The Differences in the Gospel Accounts

A simple reading of the four gospels makes the reader aware that there are differences between the accounts. They do not all give the identical stories or teachings of Jesus. At times there seems to be conflicts between the accounts. Examples:

(1) Matthew 5:1-10 vs Luke 6:20-22. *Issues:* Was Jesus' speech on a mountain or on a plain? What did he actually say? *Answers:* This may not be recording the same event. Jesus may have spoken these words several times.

(2) Matthew 20:29 vs Mark 10:46 vs Luke 18:35 *Issues:* How many blind men were there? When did the healing take place? *Answers:* Might be different events. There were both an old and a new city of Jericho. We don't have all the details.

17

Mark and Luke only refer to the blind man who spoke to Jesus.

(3) Matthew 21:1-9 vs Mark 11:1-10 vs Luke 19:29-38 *Issues:* How many animals were there? Where did they lay their cloaks? What did they shout? Answers: There were two animals. Jesus rode on the unbroken colt. Mark and Luke do not mention the one he didn't ride on. They threw cloaks both on the colt and on the ground.

(4) Matthew 26:34,69-75 Mark 14:30, 68, 72 Luke 22:34, 60-61. *Issue:* Did Jesus predict one crow or two? *Answer:* Matthew and Luke give a brief summary of what Jesus predicted. Rooster crowing means sunrise. Mark's record is more detailed. Before the rooster finished its crowing, Peter had denied Jesus three times.

1) Each author emphasizes a different aspect of the life of Jesus to a different audience..

Matthew presents Jesus as a King to his primarily Jewish audience.

Mark presents Jesus as Servant to his Roman audience.

Luke presents Jesus as the ideal man to his Greek audience.

John presents Jesus as God to his Gentile audience.

2) Each author has a distinct purpose. Luke and John say what their purpose is:

Luke 1:1-4, John 20:30-31

3) Each author has a different format. None of the gospels is a complete biography.

The chronological sequence of events is not the primary factor in the structure of the books apart from Luke. Luke 1:1-4. Authors select stories to fit their purpose. It is theological history.

2. How did the Gospels come into being?

   1) Wrong views

   (1) The gospels are the product of the church, purely man-made, with errors and contradictions. They were shaped by many people over time to prove what the church wanted to prove.

(Liberal, Secular view)

(2) The books were dictated word by word by God.

2) Factors

(1) The superintending work of the Holy Spirit in accordance with the promises of Christ. John 14:26, 16:13, 2 Tim. 3:16, 2 Peter 1:21, 1 Corinthians 2:13, 14:37, 1 Timothy 5:18, 2 Peter 3:16

(2) Oral tradition.

(3) Dependence on each other, especially on Mark.

(4) Eyewitness reports and interviews. Luke 1:1-3, 2 Peter 1:17-21, 1 John 1:1

(5) Recorded writings. Logia-sayings of Jesus. Testimonia-collections of prophetic fulfillments, earlier unpreserved gospels (We have no concrete evidences that such existed)

3) The church recognized the innate authority of the Gospels. Certain principles guided the church in this:

Does the book have innate authority?

Does the book come from an Apostle or associate of the Apostles?

Does the book have life-containing spiritual power?

Has the book been received, collected and used by the universal church?

Does the book agree with the rest of the Scriptures?

3. The Story of the Gospels

1) The Early Life of Jesus Christ. [4 b.c. to AD 27]

   (1) His birth. Matthew 1:18-25, Luke 1:5-2:20

   (2) First days in Bethlehem. Luke 2:21-38,
      Matthew 2:1-12

   (3) Sojourn in Egypt Matthew 2:13-20

   (4) Growing up in Nazareth. Matt. 2:21-23, Luke
      2:39-52

2) The Beginning of Jesus' Ministry [AD 27-30]
   3 $^{1/2}$ years]

   (1) His introduction by John the Baptist.
      John 1:14, 26-27, 29-36

   (2) His baptism. Luke 3:21-22, Mark 1:9-11,

Matthew 3:13-17

(3) His temptation. Luke 4:1-13, Matthew 4:1-11,
Mark 1:12-13

3) His initial ministry in Judea. John 1:35-50,
2:13-

3:36

4) His early ministry in Galilee and Samaria.
John 2:1-12, 4:1-42

5) His major ministry in Galilee. Luke 4:14-9:50,
John 4:43-8:59, Matthew 4:12-18:35, Mark 1:14-
9:50

(1) Rejected in Nazareth Luke. 4:16-30

(2) Headquartered in Capernaum. Luke 4:31,
Mark 2: 1

(3) Called the Apostles (Matthew 10:1-4, Mark
3:13-19, Luke 6:12-16)

(4) Preached the Sermon on the Mount
(Matthew

5-7)

[During this time which covered more than two

years Jesus made at least two trips to Jerusalem,

during feast days – John 5:1 and 7:10.]

(5) His ministry prior to choosing the Twelve. Luke 4:14-6:11

(6) From the choosing of the Twelve to his departure for Jerusalem Luke 6:12-9:50

6) His ministry on the way to Jerusalem. Luke 9:51-19:27, Matthew 19:120:34, Mark 10:1-45

7) The Final Week: His Passion. Matthew 21:1-27:66, Mark 11:1-15:47, Luke 19:28-23:56, John 12:1-19:4 Saturday - arrival in Bethany

Sunday - Triumphant entry into Jerusalem

Monday - Cleansing the temple

Tuesday - final messages, curing of the fig tree

Wednesday - Fig tree discovered, message on the Mt of Olives (Mt 24-25)

Thursday - Last Supper, Upper room discourse (John 13-17), betrayal, arrest, hearings Friday - Trial before Pilate and Herod, crucifixion, burial

Saturday - In the grave

Sunday - Resurrection

8) His Resurrection and appearances. Matthew 28: 1-20, Mark 16:1-8, Luke 24:1-53, John 20:1-21:25

4. Notable Aspects of the life of Jesus Christ

1) His teaching.

(1) Major addresses

    a. Sermon on The Mount Matthew 5-7

    b. The Olivet Discourse Mathew. 24-25

    c. The Upper Room Discourse John. 13-17

    (2) He presented himself as the one sent from God with God's Word

    (3) He taught with authority. Mark 1 :22, Mattthew 7:29, Luke 4:32.

    (4) He taught with divine wisdom. John. 7:15

    (5) He taught the necessity of radical commitment.

    (6) He taught as a prophet-calling people to repent.

2) His miracles. Their purpose was to authenticate his words and meet people's needs. Luke 4:16-21

John. 7:31, 15:22-23, Purpose: John 20:30-31, Matthew 11:20, John 14:11. Response: Matthew 12:24-32, John 2:23-25, 12:37-43

3) His parables. Definition: a parable is a story told to teach a lesson or truth.

Their purpose:

(1) To reveal spiritual truth and to illustrate it for

those who were open to it.

(2) To conceal spiritual truth from those who had

rejected it. Matthew 13:10-16, Mark. 4:21-25

4) His transfiguration. Matthew 17:1-8, Luke 9:28-36

5) His conflicts with the Jewish religious leaders.

6) His training of the Twelve.

7) His arrest, trial, crucifixion and death

8) His resurrection.

9) The importance of the record of Jesus' earthly life.

(1) It proved the truth of his claim to be sinless. Mark 2:1-12, John 8:46

(2) It proved the truth of his claim to be God

(3) It furnishes us with an example to follow:

 humility - Philippians 2:5, love - 1 John 2:6,7

(4) It provides us with the content of his teaching.

 (5) It shows how he fulfilled prophecy. e.g. Daniel

 9:24-27.

5. A Chronology of the Events of Christ's Passion

In the Upper Room Preparation for the Passover Matthew 26:17-19

Passover meal began Luke 22:17-18

Jesus washes the disciples' feet. John 13:1-20

Jesus announces his betrayal Luke 22: 21-22 Matthew 26: 21 Mark 14:18 John 13:21

Discussion of the identity of the betrayer Luke 22:23 Matthew 26:22-25, Mark 14: 19-21, John 13: 22-26

Giving of the sop to Judas John 13:26

Departure of Judas from the Upper Room John 13:27-30

Jesus' statement about his glorification John 13:31-35

Institution of the Lord's Supper Luke 22:19-20, Matthew 26:26-30, Mark 14:22-25

Announcement of Peter's denials John 13:36-38

Jesus' words of comfort John 14:1-31

The hymn Matthew 26:30, Mark 14:26

On the Way from the Upper Room to Gethsemane

Discussion about greatness Luke 22: 24-30

Discussion of Peter's denials Luke 22:31-38, Matthew 26: 31-35, Mark 14: 27-31

(At this point they leave the city and enter the Kidron Valley, Luke 22:39)

Jesus' lengthy discussion with the disciples and prayer to the Father John 15:1-17:26

Crossing the Kidron into Gethsemane John 18:1

The Prayer of Gethsemane Luke 22:39-46, Matthew 26: 36-46, Mark 14:32-42

Betrayal by Judas Luke 22:47-53, Matthew 26:47-56, Mark 14:43-49, John 18: 2-12

Disciples flee Matthew 26: 56, Mark 14:50-52

The Trials of Jesus

Hearing before Annas John 18:12-24

Peter's denials take place during these two hearings.

Hearing before Caiaphas Luke 22:54-65, Matthew 26:57-68, Mark 14:54-65

Peter's denials Luke 22: 54-62, Matthew 26:58, 69-71, Mark 14:54, 66-72, John 18: 15-18, 25-27

Formal Indictment by the Counsel Matthew 27: 1, Mark 15:1, Luke 22: 66-71

Trial before Pilate Luke 23:1-7 13-25, Matthew 27:2-26, Mark 15:2-15, John 18:28-19:16

Trial before Herod Luke 23: 8-12 This interview is preceded and followed by Pilate's inquests

Mocking by Pilate's soldiers Matthew 27:27-31, Mark 15:16-20

On the Way to Calvary

Simon carries the cross Luke 23:26, Matthew 27:3,2 Mark 15:21 (Jesus carries the cross-beam until he is wearied) John 19:17

Jesus' words to the women Luke 23 27-31

On the Cross

Jesus placed on the cross Luke 23:33, Mark 15:24 (3rd hour), Matthew 27:35

His Garments divided by the soldiers. John 19:18-24

Wine and gall offered Matthew 27:33,34, Mark 15:23

"Father, forgive them" Luke 23:34

Jesus' words to John and Mary John 19:25-27

Mocking by soldiers and others Luke 23: 35-38, Matthew 27: 39-44, Mark 15: 29-32

Jesus' words to the repentant thief Lke 23:39-43

Three hours of darkness (6th through 9th hours) Luke 23:44-4,5 Matthew27:45, Mark 15:33

Words at about the ninth hour Mt 27:46 Mk 15:34

"Eli, eli, lama sabachthani." Matthew 27:46-50, Mark 15:34-36

"I am thirsty." He is given sour wine on a sponge. Matthew 27:48, Mark 15:36, John 19:28, 29

"It is finished" John 19:30

"Father into your hands I commit my spirit" Luke 23:46

Death of the Savior Luke 23:46, Matthew 27: 50, Mark 15:37, John 19:30

Rending of the temple veil Matthew 27:5,1 Mark 15:38

Earthquake and opening of tombs Matthew 27:52-53

Words of the centurion Luke 23:47, Matthew 27:54, Mark 15:39

Piercing of Jesus' side John 19:31-37

6. A Chronology of the Resurrection and Post-Resurrection Appearances of Christ

The resurrection of Jesus Christ

The coming of the angel(s) to roll away the stone with the attending fright of the guards Matthew 28:1-4

Arrival of Mary Magdalene at the tomb and her departure to inform Peter and John that the stone had been removed John 20:1-2

Arrival of the other women, the message of the angel(s) to them and their departure to tell the disciples the message Mark 16:1-8, Matthew 28:1,5-,8 Luke 24:1-8

Arrival of Peter and John at the tomb John 20:3-10, Luke 24:12

Appearance of Jesus to the women (minus Mary Magdalene) Matthew 28:9-10

Report of the guards to the chief priests and their bribery Matthew 28:11-15

Appearance of Jesus to Mary Magdalene at the tomb John 20:11-17

Report of the women to the disciples Luke 24:9-10

Report of Mary Magdalene to the disciples Mark 16 9-11

Appearance of Jesus to Peter Luke 24:34, 1 Cor 15:5

Appearance of Jesus to the two disciples on road to Emmaus Mark 16:14-18, Luke 24:13-35

Appearance of Jesus to the ten Apostles in the Upper Room Mark 16:14-18, Luke 24:26-39, John 20:19-23, 1 Corinthians 15:5 (Thomas missing)

Appearance of Jesus to the Eleven in the Upper Room (one week later) John 20:24-29

Appearance of Jesus to seven disciples in Galilee (at Sea of Galilee) John 21:1-23

Appearance of Jesus to over 500 believers 1 Corinthians 15:6

Appearance of Jesus to James 1 Corinthians 15:6

Appearance of Jesus in Galilee (on the mountain) with His great commission Matthew 28:16-20

The Ascension of Jesus from Mt. of Olives Mark 16:19, Luke 24: 50-51, Acts 1:4-12

(Acts tells us that Jesus appeared to his disciples periodically for a period of over forty days)

7. The Key Event of the Gospels
Each of the four Gospels is built around the record of the death and resurrection of Jesus. More than half of John is devoted to the final week of Jesus' earthly life. Jesus said that this is why he came— to die. Matthew 20:28, John 3:14.

8. The Audience of the Gospels. Apart from the first eleven chapters of John, these books were written to the Church—to true believers.

9. The Theme of the Gospels. The coming of the Messiah to fulfill the Old Testament promises to make atonement for sin and provide eternal life.

Roman Procurators of Judea, Roman Emperors, Herodian Kings, and Jewish High Priests in New Testament Times

Roman Procurators of Judea

Pontius Pilate AD 26-36 Luke 3:1, at the time of the Crucifixion of Christ

Felix AD 52-59.   Acts 21:27-24:25

Festus AD 59-61.   Acts 24:27-26:32

Roman Emperors

Augustus 27 b.c. to AD14. Luke 2:1

Tiberius AD 14-37 Luke 3:1

Caligula AD 37-41

Claudius AD 41-54. Acts 11:28, 18:2

Nero AD 54-68 Acts 25:8-10, 27:24, 2 Timothy 4:16-17

Jewish High Priests

Matthias ben Theophilus   5/4 b.c.   Matthew 2:4

Ananus ben Seth (Annas)   AD 6-15 John 18:13

Joseph Caiaphas (son-in-law of annas) AD 18-36 John 11: 49, 18:13-24, Acts 4:6

Ananias ben Nedebeus AD 46-58 Acts 22:5, 23:1-3, 24:1

Herods

Herod the Great 37 b.c. to 4 b.c. At the time of Jesus' birth. Matthew 2, Luke 1:5

Herod Archelaus 4 b.c. – AD 6(son of Herod the Great) Matthew 2:22

Herod Antipas (son of Herod the Great) 4 b.c. -AD 39. Luke 3:1, Matthew 14:1, Acts 4:27 at the time of Jesus' ministry. Killed John the Baptist. Second husband of Herodias Herod Phillip (son of Herod the Great) 4 b.c.-AD 34 Lk 3:1, 19, Matt. 6:17

First husband or Herodias

Herod Agrippa I AD 37-44   Acts 12

Herod Agrippa II AD 50s- ?? Died in AD 90's Last of the Herodian dynasty. Acts 23:35

Recommended Resources

 Kenneth E. Bailey, Jesus Through Middle Eastern Eyes, IVP, 2008

*Kenneth E. Bailey, Poet and Peasant and Through Peasant Eyes, Eerdmans, 1976

Craig Blomberg, Jesus and the Gospels: An Introduction and Survey, B&H, 2009

Darrell Bock and Benjamin I Simpson, Jesus according to Scripture, Baker, 2021

F. F. Bruce, The Hard Sayings of Jesus, IVP, 1983

D. A. Carson, The Sermon on the Mount, Baker, 1978 Stanley Ellison, Parables in the Eye of the Storm, Kregel, 2001 Robert Guelich, The Sermon on the Mount: A Foundation for Understanding, Word, 1991

Everett F. Harrison, A Short Life of Christ, Eerdmans, 1968

Harold Hoehner, Chronological Aspects of the Life of Christ, Zondervan, 1978

Gary Inrig, Parables: Understanding What Jesus Meant, Discovery House,1991

John R. W. Stott, The Message of the Sermon on the Mount, IVP, 1978

Mark L. Strauss, <u>Four Portraits of One Jesus: A Survey of Jesus and the Gospels</u>, Zondervan, 2020

A SNAPSHOT OF MATTHEW

Author

Matthew, one the Twelve Apostles

The author of this Gospel is unstated in the text but early church tradition affirms that it was Matthew one of the twelve Apostles There is also internal support in the book for this tradition: the Jewish flavor of the book, the numerical interest of the author, the inclusion of the miracle of the tax money (17:24-27), and the humble account of the feast Matthew provided for Jesus.

Date and Place of Writing

Between AD 50 and AD 70, perhaps in the 60's before the fall of Jerusalem and destruction of the temple. Perhaps it was written from Judea or Antioch.

Date of Events

4 b.c. to AD 30/33

Recipients

Matthew's intended audience would seem to have been Palestinian Jewish Christians. Matthew is a very Jewish book.

This is the report of early Christian tradition.

This is seen in the emphasis on Old Testament prophetic fulfillments.

The style, vocabulary, and subject matter are Jewish in nature.

Quotations from the Old Testament reflect the Hebrew text not the Greek translation of the Old Testament (the Septuagint).

Matthew is the only Gospel to record the resurrection of the Old Testament believers (27:52,53) and the slaughter of the infants of Bethlehem (2:1-12).

The genealogy of Jesus given in Matthew 1 is built around Abraham and David.

Jewish customs are not explained (15:2 vs Mark 7:3-4) Compare 14:1,21:1,22 with
Luke 2:1-2 and 3:1, 2.

Purpose

Matthew lays out the life and teachings of Jesus as a framework for Christian faith and mission.

He shows the identity and work of Jesus Christ the Savior in order to:

1. provide apologetic and evangelistic material for witness and to encourage that witness.

2. prove that Jesus is the promised Messiah and thus to draw people to faith in Him.

3. explain to Jewish believers the change in God's kingdom program and inclusion of the Gentiles in the Church to foster acceptance of the Gentiles and unity in the church.

4. call believers into a life of discipleship - a teaching manual for the church to bring believers' lives into conformity with the purposes and mission of Jesus.

Theme

Jesus Christ is King and Lord of all. He is the Son of David [1:1] and has all authority [28:18]

The Story

Matthew began his story with the announcement to Joseph that Mary, by the power of the Holy Spirit, will give birth to the Messiah and Savior.

He tells of the visit of the Magi and the flight of Mary and Joseph to Egypt. He informs us of the ministry of John the Baptist, the baptism of Jesus, his temptation by Satan and his calling of his first disciples. In chapters 4 through 7 Matthew records the teaching Jesus proclaimed to his disciples on a mountain in Galilee. Chapters 8-11 emphasize the healing ministry of Jesus, and the sending out of the Twelve. Chapters 11-13 highlight the growing opposition to Jesus by the Jewish religious leaders and his kingdom parables. Chapter 15 records the execution of John the Baptist, the Feeding of the Five Thousand and the story of Jesus walking on the water. Chapters 16-20 record further miracles and teachings, the increased tension with the religious leaders and the unveiling of his glory before Peter, James and John. In chapter 21 Jesus formally presents himself as the messianic king, cleanses the temple and tells several more parables. Chapters 22-23 again focus on the conflict with the religious leaders and Jesus' pronouncement of woe upon them. In Chapter 24 and 25 Matthew records Jesus' prophetic message dealing with the end of the age. Chapters 26-27 records the last days of Jesus life, including his Passover meal with the Twelve, his prayer in Gethsemane, his betrayal by Judas, hearings before Caiaphas and Pilate, his mocking, crucifixion, death, and burial. Chapter 28 is the resurrection story and the giving of the great commission of Jesus to his disciples.

Outline

1. Credentials of the King 1:1-2:23
2. Authentication of the King 3:1-4:11
3. Message of the King 4:12-11:1

   Presented 4:12-7:29

   Proved 8:1-9:34

   Multiplied 9:35-11:1
4. Opposition to the King 11:2-13:53
5. Rejection of the King 14:1-27:61

   Rejection 14:1-25:46

   Crucifixion 26:1-27:66

6. Resurrection of the King 28:1-20

5. Reaction of the King. 13:54-19:2

[This outline reflects the teaching of John Masters]

1. Incarnation and Preparation. 1:1-4:11

2. Principles of the King 4:12-7:29

3. Manifestation of the King 8:1-11:1

4. Opposition to the King 11:2-13:53

5. Reaction of the King 13:543-19:2

6. Final Presentation and rejection of the King
   19:3-26:2

7. Crucifixion and Resurrection of the King.
{This outline reflects the teaching of Stanley
Toussaint and is based on the repeated phrase
"when he (Jesus) had finished (7:28, 11:1, 13:53,
19:1, 26:1)]

1. Matthew is a story. It is a historical narrative. It
tells a story of real people and real events, It is
biographical narrative but not a biography. It is
narrative told with theological purpose.

43

2. Matthew tells a unique story. 35% of Mathew is only found in Matthew.

3. The theme of Jewish rejection is a key thought throughout the book. Only Matthew records the Jewish acceptance of responsibility for Christ's death (27:24-25). Only Matthew recorded the Jewish leaders' explanation of the empty tomb (28:11-15 cf. 21:43)

4. Matthw emphasized the mission of Jesus as a fulfillment of God's prophetic plan 1:23; 2:5-6, 15:2:18, 23, 3:3; 4:15-16, 8:17, 12:18-21, 13:35, 21:5, and 27:9

5. Matthew gives the Gentiles a place in his story: 2:1-12 8:5-12, 15:21-28, 21:43, 28:19-20

6. Only Matthew mentions the Church 16:18, 18:17

7. Matthew puts emphasis on the teachings of Christ. Five major discourses: 5:3-7:27,10:5-42, 13:3-52, 18:3-35 and 24:2-25 These messages comprise 60% of the book. The story sections in Matthew are shorter than Mark's

8. Matthew is developed only generally chronologically. He groups incidents, miracles, parables, and sayings. He has alternate sections of teaching and activities. Chapters 1-4 are generally chronological. Chapters 5-13 are topical. Chapters 14-28 are generally chronological.

9. Every new phase in the life of Jesus is preceded in Matthew by an account of a parallel phase in the life of his forerunner, John the Baptist.

10. Matthew emphasized the return of King Jesus to judge and to rule sat the end of the age.

11. Matthew emphasized the mission Jesus gave his disciples to proclaim the Gospel and make disciples. 10:1-42, 28:18-20

Major Applications

1. To unbeleivers. It would be especially good to have Jewish people read Matthew as their introduction to Jesus Christ.

2. Matthew is helpful in understanding how the Old Testament and New Testament fit together

3. The authority of the Lord Jesus Christ is a key application. He is the King. He calls us to discipleship and to his mission,

4. Assurance that Jesus is the Christ who came to give His life as a ransom.

5. Matthew is an important book to study for knowledge of the teachings of Christ. How often we evangelicals escape to Paul instead of sitting at the feet of the Lord Jesus Himself!

Recommended Resources

Craig L. Blomberg, Matthew, [NAC] Broadman, 1992

*D. A. Carson, The Expositor's Bible Commentary, Volume 8. Zondervan

R. T. France, The Gospel of Matthew, [NICNT] Eerdmans

Craig S. Keener, A Commentary on the Gospel of Mathew, 1999

Leon Morris, The Gospel According to Matthew, Eerdmans 1992

Grant Osbourne and Clinton Arnold, Matthew, [ECNT], Zondervan, 2010

Stanley Toussaint, Behold the King: A Study of Matthew, Multnomah Press, 199

A Snapshot of Mark

Author

Mark, the companion of Paul and Peter. The author of this gospel is not stated in the text, but early church tradition affirms that it was John Mark, a cousin of Barnabas. Some suggest that Mark is based on the preaching and teaching of the Apostle Peter. Acts 12:12, 25, 13:5:13, 15:36-41, Colossians 4:10-11, 2 Timothy 4:11, Philemon 24, 1 Peter 5:13.

Date and Place of Writing

Mark was probably written in the early to middle AD 60's, shortly before the deaths of Paul and Peter and probably from Rome.

Date of the Events of the Story

4 b.c. to AD 30/33

Recipients

Roman believers or at least Gentile believers who were not from Palestine. Evidence for this conclusion is found in:

(1) The explanations of Jewish customs and geography of Palestine 7:2-3, 212:42, 13:3,

(2) Few Old Testament quotations. 1:2-3, 4:12, 7:6-7, 11:9, 10, 17, 12:10, 36,

(3) Little mention of the Law, 12:19, 26, 28, 31, 10:5, 19,

(4) Presence of Latinisms (Latin words written with Greek letters) 14:65, 15:15, 19, 21,

(5) Explanations of Aramaic words (Aramaic was the spoken language of the Jews in Palestine) 7:34, 5:41, 14:36,

(6) Other Latin words 3:6, 4:21, 5:9, 14, 6: 27, 37, 7:4, 12: 14, 42, 15:15, 16, 39, 44,

(7) The mention of Alexander and Rufus Mark 15:21, Romans 16:13.

Purpose

1. To present an essential outline of the story of Jesus. Mark 1:1 serves as a title for the book.

2. To encourage the listener to follow Jesus as a disciple, one whose faith is characterized by self-denial, sacrifice and service.

3. To encourage suffering Christians in Rome by the example of the rejection and suffering of Jesus as God's Servant.

Theme

The good news of Jesus Christ, the Messianic Son of God and Suffering Servant.

The Story

Mark begins his story of Jesus with the ministry of John the Baptist, the baptism and temptation of Jesus and the calling his first disciples and omits the birth narratives found in Matthew and Luke. For the most part Mark lays out the same progression of the ministry of Jesus as do Matthew and Luke.

Some believe this shorter version of the story was a foundational resource for Matthew and Luke. Mark ends with the story of the resurrection of Jesus. Most evangelical scholars do not believe that Mark 16:9-20 were a part of Mark's original manuscript.

Outline

[Note: All outlines are somewhat arbitrary. Mark probably did not start with an outline as he wrote.]

1. Introduction 1:1-13

2. Jesus' Ministry in Galilee: Rejection. 1:14-9:50

   He is acclaimed. 1:14-45

   He is opposed 2:1-3:6

   He is rejected 3:7-6:6

   [The parable of the sower in 4:1-20 explains this

   rejection]

Ministry of the Twelve 6:7-8:26

2. Preparation for his passion. 8:27-9:50 [Many Bible teachers see 8:26 as a key divider in Mark and 8:27-9:50 as a bridge or transitional section.]

3. Jesus' Ministry in Perea: Rejection 10:1-52

4. Jesus' Ministry in Jerusalem: Rejection 11:1-16:8

Rejected 11:1-13:37 [Chapter 13 explains the consequences of the Jewish rejection of Jesus]

Crucified 14:1-15:27

Risen 16:1-8

[Mark 16:9-20 were probably not an original part of Mark 's Gospel.]

Characteristics and Points of Interest

1. The emphasis of Mark is on the works of Jesus not his words. Mark is the shortest Gospel.

It is generally chronological. It is a story. As people in those times were generally illiterate the story was narrated. The action is fast. Mark uses the word "immediately" 41 times.

2. Mark presents Jesus as both the authoritative Messianic Son of God (1:1,11, 3:11, 5:7, 15:39), and the suffering Servant (2:10, 28, 8:28, 31, 38, 9:9, 12, 31, 10:33, 45, 13:26, 14:21, 41, 62).

3. Mark has an emphasis on the "gospel." 1:1, 14, 15, 8:35, 10:29, 13:10, and 14:9.

The good news that the promised kingdom has arrived.

4. The cross is central in Mark. One-third of the book deals with the crucifixion.

5. The center of the story is conflict. The main antagonists are: Jesus, the religious leaders, the disciples and the crowd. There are also minor characters. The religious leaders reject Jesus, leading to the crucifixion. The disciples are projected as believing in him but unable to understand either his mission or the nature of discipleship. The crowd is initially well-disposed

toward Jesus but without faith eventually reject him.

6. In Mark there is a call to discipleship, which involves faith which is seen in self-denial, sacrifice and humble service.

Major Applications

Mark gives us the essentials of the story of Jesus and as such is good book to suggest to seekers and young believers.

Mark helps us to understand discipleship and deepen our discipleship.

Mark can encourage rejected or persecuted Christians.

Recommended Resources

Kenneth Bailey, <u>Jesus Through Middle Eastern Eyes</u>, IVP

Stanley A. Ellison, <u>Parables in the Eye of the Storm</u>, Kregel

R. T. France, <u>The Gospel of Mark</u>, [NIGTC] Eerdmans, 2002

*Abraham Kuruvilla, <u>Mark</u>, Cascade Books, 2012

Robert H. Stein, <u>Mark</u>, [ECNT] Baker, 2008

Mark Strauss And Clinton E. Arnold, <u>Mark</u>, [ECNT] Zondervan, 2014

A SNAPSHOT OF LUKE

Author

Luke, a physician and companion of Paul.

The author of this Gospel is not stated in the text, but both evidence from within the book and the support of early church tradition point to Dr. Luke. [Colossians 4:14] Luke was not an eyewitness, but he had access to eyewitnesses, as well as written sources under the guidance of the Holy Spirit. One internal evidence is the presence of much medical terminology in the book. There are up to 400 medical terms peculiar to Luke. Luke is also the only one to record the healing of the ear cut off by Peter. Luke was most likely a Gentile.

Date of Writing

Around AD 62. Luke is part I of Luke-Acts and Acts was probably written before the end of Paul's Roman imprisonment in AD 62 because his release is not mentioned in Acts.

Date of Events

4 B.C.to AD 30/33

Recipients

Greek speaking Gentiles

Purpose

To set forth an orderly, accurate, and detailed account of Jesus Christ as the Savior in order to give the readers, Greek speaking Gentile Christians, assurance as to the historical accuracy and basis of their faith. Luke also wants his readers to know who Jesus Christ was, the way to salvation, and the duties of discipleship. He is also explaining the inclusion of Gentiles in the new community of Jesus' followers.

Theme

The Salvation of Jesus Christ, the Son of Man.

There is a great emphasis on Jesus as Savior. This is seen in the great use of the words "save, salvation, lost, repent." Key Text: Luke 19:10

There is also an emphasis on Christ's humanity. This is seen in his genealogy, tracing his ancestry through Mary back to Adam, in the details about His daily contacts with people, and in his perfect obedience to his Father's will, which qualified him to be the Savior.

The Story

Luke begins his story with the announcements of the coming births of John the Baptist and Jesus.

He tells the story of Jesus' birth, circumcision and presentation at the temple. He alone tells the story of Jesus talking with the rabbinic teachers in the temple at age 12. He relates the account of John's ministry, the baptism and temptation of Jesus, his rejection in Nazareth and his choosing of the Apostles. Chapters 4-9 record his miracles and teachings in Galilee. In 9:51 Luke begins the account of Jesus' final journey to Jerusalem. This includes miracles, teaching, and many parables unique to Luke. Chapters 19-23 record in final days in Jerusalem, his debates with the religious rulers, his prophetic teaching, last Passover, prayer in Gethsemane, his betrayal, arrest, inquisitions before the Sanhedrin, Pilate and Herod, crucifixion, death, and burial. Chapter 24 includes his resurrection, post-resurrection appearances and ascension.

Outline

1. Prologue 1:1-4

2. Preparation of the Son of Man. 1:5-4:13

3. Ministry of the Son of Man .4:14-21:38

   In Galilee 4:14-9:50

   Toward Jerusalem 9:51-19:27

   In Jerusalem 19:28-21:38

 4. The Death of the Son of Man. 22:1-23:56

 5.The Victory of the Son of Man 24:1-53

Characteristics and Points of Interest

1. Most of Luke 9:51-18:14 is unique to Luke's Gospel. 485 of Luke's 1,151 verses are unique to his gospel.

2. There are many sub-themes in Luke: the universality of salvation (Jesus is shown not only as the Jewish Messiah but as Savior of the world (3:4-6), the rejection of the Savior, importance of individual people including women, children, the poor, and the despised, the Holy Spirit, the purpose of God as fulfilled by Christ, praise and worship (the book begins and ends in the temple) and the call and cost of discipleship.

3. Luke is of the best Greek in the N.T. It is rich in vocabulary There are over 750 words used in Luke that are not found in the rest of the New Testament.

4. Luke was a Gentile writing to Gentiles. He never used the Jewish title Rabbi. He substituted Greek names for Hebrew ones. He explained Jewish customs. He traced Jesus' ancestry to

Adam. He quoted the Greek translation of the Old Testament.

5. Luke is the gospel most concerned to present an orderly, generally chronological history. He refers to secular historical events to date the events recorded in this Gospel. [1:5, 2:1, 2, 3:1]

Yet, Luke, like all other biblical historians writes theological history: Real, accurate historical facts written to convey spiritual truth. He is selective in what he writes, yet the most comprehensive of the three synoptic gospels (Matthew, Mark, and Luke). Six of the twenty miracles recorded by Luke are only recorded by Luke.

6. Luke 10:7 is quoted by Paul in 1Timothy 5:18 as being Scripture on a parallel with the Old Testament.

7. Luke is the first volume of a two-part composition, with Acts being volume 2. Acts 1:1

8. Luke puts emphasis on the teaching ministry of Jesus. Eighteen of the twenty-three parables recorded by Luke are unique to Luke's Gospel.

Major Applications

For assurance--our faith is based on events which really took place. The words and actions of Jesus are authentic and carefully investigated and recorded.

Luke shows us Jesus as our example.

Luke shows us the nature and basis of salvation.

Luke shows us the importance, the duties, and the cost of discipleship.

Luke shows us the importance of worship, prayer and witness in the life of a disciple.

Recommended Resources

Thabiti Anyabwile, Exalting Jesus in Luke, IVP, 2018

Kenneth E. Bailey, Jesus Through Middle Eastern Eyes, IVP, 2008

Kenneth L. Bailey, <u>Poet and Peasant and Through Peasant Eyes</u>, Eerdmans, 1976, 1980

*Darrell L. Bock, <u>Luke</u>, [2 volumes] Baker, 19943

Joel B. Green, <u>The Gospel of Luke</u>, [NICNT] Eerdmans, 1997

I. Howard Marshall, <u>Commentary on Luke</u>, Eerdmans, 1978

A SNAPSHOT OF JOHN

Author

Though the author of this book is not identified in the book itself, early Christian tradition uniformly says John, the Apostle was the author. There is no credible reason to doubt this tradition. The author was close to Jesus (John 13:23-24).

It would only seem likely that John, who was one of the inner core of three disciples, would write an account. John was the son of Zebedee and a professional fisherman on the Sea of Galilee. Along with his brother James he became one of the earliest of Jesus disciples (Mark 1:19-20). It is quite likely that he was, in fact, a cousin of Jesus (compare Mark 16: l; Matthew 27:56 and John 19:25).

Date and Place of Writing

The book of John was probably written between AD 85 and AD 95. It was probably written from

Ephesus on the west coast of the Roman province of Asia which we know today as Turkey.

Purpose

The author clearly states his purpose for writing this book in chapter 20:30-31: "Jesus did many other miraculous signs in the presence of his disciples, which are not recorded in this book. But these are written that you may believe that Jesus is the Christ, the son of God, and that by believing you may have life in his name." [NIV] However, his purpose does not seem to be only evangelistic. There is much truth here intended for the edification of the followers of Jesus Christ.

The Story

John begins his story with the witness of John the Baptist to Jesus and the calling of the first disciples. Only John reports on the earliest ministries of Jesus in Judea and Galilee [the wedding in Cana, the first cleansing of the temple, the interview with Nicodemus, and the Samaritan woman at the well]. John records a number of miracles and much teaching of Jesus unique to John as well as his debates with the religious teachers. John 12 begins John's account of the last week of Jesus' earthly life. John uniquely records the account of his washing the disciples' feet [13:1-20], his words of instruction to them [13:21-16:33], and his prayer for them [17:1-26]. In his account of the arrest, trials and crucifixion of Jesus, John uniquely records the grounding of the arresting party, the pre-trial before Annas the high priest emeritus, some of the dialogue between Jesus and Pilate, and the involvement of Nicodemus in his burial. In the resurrection account in chapters 20-21 John tells the story of the encounter of Mary Magdalene with the risen Jesus, the doubting of Thomas, and the meeting with seven of the Apostles in Galilee.

Outline

The first twelve chapters of this book are developed around seven miraculous signs. The book has five units.

1. The Introductory Prologue 1:1-51

2. The Book of Seven Signs 2:1-12:50

3. Jesus' farewell address to his disciples. 13:1 17:26

4. Jesus and resurrection. 18:1-20:29

5. The Epilogue 20:30-21:25

Characteristics and Points of Interest

1. John is different in many ways from Matthew, Mark and Luke. 93% of the content of John is not found in the other Gospels.

2. John fixes the duration of Jesus' public ministry to about 3 and 1/2 years [2:13, 5:1, 6:4, 11:55] 2:13 mentions Jesus' first Passover visit. Here is John's chronology: (1) From his introduction by John to the first Passover 1:29-2:12.

This was a few months, part of a year.

(2) The first full year of ministry. 2:13-5:1

[This assumes that the feast of 5:1 is a Passover]

(3) Second full year-Passover to Passover 5:1-6:4.

(4) Third full year, Passover to Passover 6:5-20:29

(5) Post resurrection time. [Acts 1:3 says that this was 40 days] 20:20-21:24.]

3. The structure of John 1-12 is formed around the seven miraculous signs. The teachings are clustered around the seven signs and interpret the signs in terms of spiritual truth. John shows how these miracles with their associated teachings drew out two responses: faith or rejection of faith.

4. Some of the key words and concepts in John include: Believe (words for faith used 93 times) The identity of Jesus 1:1, 14, 3:13, 8:58-59, 9:38, 10:28-30, 12:45 Eternal Life 3:16, 17, 36, 4:14, 36, 5:24, 6:27, 40, 47, 51, 54, 68, 10:10, 12:25, 50, 17:2, 3

The Word 1:1,14, 2:22; 3:34; 4:50; 5:38, 6:68, 8:31,52, 10:35, 12;38 48-50, 14:24, 15:3, 7, 20, 25, 17:6-8, 14, 17, 18:9, 32

Light/darkness 1:4, 3:19-21, 35, 5:35, 8:12, 9:5, 11:9-10, 12:35-36, 46

The claims of Jesus 6:35, 46, 8:12, 10:7-9, 11, 14, 25, 12:45, 14:6, 15:1,5

God's sovereignty.6:37, 39, 44-45, 65, 8:47, 10:26-27, 12:37-40, 12:37-40, 15:16, 17:6

5. The mission of Jesus in John's Gospel

1) To give light to every man. 1:9, 12:46

2) To reveal God. 1:18, 17:6

3) To take away the sins of the world. 1:29

4) To give eternal life to those who believe 3:14-16, 9:33, 10:10

5) To save the world. 3:17, 12:47

6) To do the will of God. 4:34, 5:30, 6:39-40, 17:4, 6, 26.

7) For judgment. 9:39

8) To lay down his life. 19:11, 15, 17, 18

9) To die. 12:27

10) To say what God told him to say. 12:50, 17:8

11) To set an example. 13:15

12) To testify to the truth. 18:37

6. Five key facts about the sign miracles

1) These seven miracles illustrate seven truths about Jesus and his mission. They are object lessons.

2) Each miracle (or pair of miracles) is followed by explicit teaching, teaching the truth illustrated by the miracle. The sixth sign 8:12-10:42 is an exception where the sign is encased before and after with the teaching.

3) Each miracle arises out of a situation of need whose solution lies beyond human ability.

4) Each miracle provokes responses. Each is a crisis point drawing people toward a decision, either belief or rejection.

7. One focus in John is on Jesus' coming and going. The prologue says he was eternally with God [1:2]. Chapters 1-12 focus on his coming: the

questions of who he is, where he came from and what he came to do are the focus. [3:13, 31, 6:32-33, 8:14, 23, 43, 6:33, 38, 41, 42, 50, 51, 57-58, 16;27-30]. Chapters 13-21 focus on his going: his return to the Father, what he will have accomplished, and what this mean for his disciples. [6:62, 7:33, 8:14, 21,22, 13:1, 3, 33, 36, 14:2-4, 12, 28, 16:5, 7, 10, 17, 28, 20:17]

8. The ultimate rejection (the crucifixion) becomes the ultimate focus of the faith which results in eternal life.

Major Applications

1. To appeal to people to believe in Jesus in order to obtain eternal life. 20:30-31

2. To assure believers of who Jesus is and what he accomplished.

3. To encourage believers to live as Jesus commanded his disciples to live.

Recommended Resources

F. F. Bruce, The Gospel of John, Eerdmans, 1983

*D. A. Carson, The Gospel According to John, Eerdmans, 1991

D. A. Carson, The Farewell Discourse and Final Prayer of Jesus, Baker, 1980

Craig S. Keener, The Gospel of John, (2 Vols), Hendrickson, 2010

J. Ramsay Michaels, The Gospel of John, [NICNT] Eerdmans, 2010

A SNAPSHOT OF ACTS

Author

Luke. [Luke 1:1-4, Acts 1:1]   Acts is part 2 of Luke.

Date and Place of Writing

@ AD 63 probably from Rome

Historical scope

AD 30-AD 62

Recipients

A Gentile believer, Theophilus and the Church in general

Purpose

To show the orderly and sovereignly directed progress of the Gospel from Jerusalem to Rome, (the center of the world) (from the Jews to the

Gentiles) thus to confirm faith and to assure believers that the foundation of their faith is firm.

Theme

The progress of the development of the church.

Key verse: Acts 1:8

There are many sub-themes in the book (These will be noted under characteristics)

The average believer approaches Acts as the history book of the early church. He reads it to discover what happened. This is an inadequate approach.

Acts is theological history intended to edify and challenge us.

The Story

Acts begins with the final words of Jesus to his disciples and his ascension back to heaven. Luke tells us of the replacement of Judas with Matthias and the coming of the Holy Spirit to indwell and empower the Church. Luke shows us how the Church began to grow and how it spread to Judea and Samaria in the midst of growing opposition.

He reports on the martyrdom of Stephen, the ministry of Phillip to an Ethiopian, and the conversion and calling of Saul [Paul].

Chapter 10 & 11 relate the conversion of the first Gentiles, Cornelius and his household and how Peter explained it to the Jewish believers in Jerusalem. Beginning with chapter 13 the focus is on Paul and the expansion of the Gospel to the Roman world. Luke records the three missionary journeys of Paul and his companions [13-20] and the great church council in Jerusalem [15]. Chapters 21-28 tell of Paul's arrest in Jerusalem, incarceration in Caesarea, his journey to Rome and his Roman imprisonment. The book ends with Paul's two-year house confinement and his continued witness.

Outline

1. The Witness in Jerusalem: The Church founded 1:1-6: 7

2. The Witness in Judea and Samaria: The church expanded 6: 8-9: 31

3. The Witness to the Gentiles: Climax of Peter's witness 9:32-12:24

    1) A New Missionary Principle 9:32-11:18

    2) A New Missionary Center 11: 19-30

    3) A New Missionary Vitality 12: 1-24

  4. The Witness Extended to Asia: Establishment of Paul as witness. 12:25-16:5

    (1) Confirmation of Paul's Mission 12: 25-13: 52

    (2) Characterization of Paul's Mission 14: 1-23

    (3) Consolidation of Paul's Mission 14: 24-16:5

5. The Witness Extended to Aegean Area: Christ Jesus exalted among the Gentiles.16:6-19:20

  1) The Spirit Sovereignly Seeks Souls 16: 5-40

2) The Spirit Sovereignly Selects Localities 17:1-

   18:17

3) The Spirit is Sovereign in Sequence of Events

   18:18-9:20

6. The Witness Extended to Rome 19:21-28:31

1) Repudiation of Paul' s Witness in Jerusalem 19:23-23:10

2) Relocation of Paul's Witness to Rome 23:11-28:31

[This outline is based on one developed by Professor Zane Clark Hodges, Dallas Seminary. It is built around summaries of progress found throughout the book.]

Characteristics and Points of Interest

1. A major purpose of Acts was to defend Paul 's apostleship and the extension of Gospel to the Gentiles.

2. Some key ideas of the Book

1) Witness. (a technical term, usually applied strictly to the Apostles and Paul). [1:8, 6:3, 10:22, 43, 13:22, 14:3, 15:8, 16:2, 22:5,12, 23:11 26: 5, etc.

2) The Kingdom [1:6, 8:12, 14:22, 19: 8, 20:25, 28:23, 31]

3) The Universality of the Gospel. [1:8, 9:15, 10:1-18, 11:1-18, 13:46-48, 14:27, 15:6-9, 17:26, 18:6, 26:23, 28:28].

3. Acts 1:8 is not a command but a prediction which unfolds in the book.

4. The sovereign purpose of God in creating the Church and bringing the Gospel to the ends of the earth is seen in various ways in Acts.

1) The will and purpose of God is directly stated. 2:23, 39, 4:27, 28, 13:48

2) The progress of the Gospel fulfilled OT prophecy. Luke 24: 47, Acts 1:4-8, 20, 2:16-21, 3:24, 10:43, 13:40, 47, 15:15-18, 28:25-28

3) The emphasis on the enabling ministry of the Holy Spirit including the display of sign and wonders.

4) Persecution could not defeat God's purpose.

5) The specific directions given to the missionaries by God.

5. Jewish rejection and its consequences including the inclusion of the Gentiles

6. The comparison of the ministry of Peter and the Apostles with that of Paul. Peter predominates to 12:24; Paul in remainder of the book. So, a sub-purpose was to demonstrate that Paul's mission to the Gentiles was a legitimate extension and development of the Gospel. There is a shift from a Jewish to a Gentile focus.

7. Witness is to the reality of the death, the resurrection and ascension of Jesus.

8. Benefits of receiving Christ stressed are forgiveness and the indwelling Spirit.

9. Explains how the universal Church arose from the few Jewish followers of Jesus.

10. "We" sections are when Luke was with Paul. [16:10-17, 20: 5-15, 21:1-18, Chapters 27 and 28].

11. Luke provides his readers with regular progress reports. [1:15, 2:41, 47, 44, 5:14, 6:7, 8:12, 9:31, 42, 12:24, 13:49, 14:21, 16:6, 17:4, 12, 18:34, 18:8, 19:10, 20].

Major Applications

1. Assurance: The foundation of our faith stands firm. The progress of the Gospel will continue in spite of opposition. (Matthew 16:18 "I will build my church-gates of hell will not overcome it."

2. Examples for edification and motivation: Of how the church is to function and grow. Of how missions and evangelism are accomplished.

Of how a witness behaves (Stephen, Philip, Peter, Paul)

One intention of Luke was to show the Christlikeness of the witnesses.

Recommended Resources

*Darrell L. Bock, <u>Acts</u>, [ECNT] Baker, 2007

F. F. Bruce, <u>Paul: Apostle of the Heart Set Free</u>, Eerdmans, 1977

I. Howard Marshall, <u>The Acts of the Apostles</u>, Eerdmans, 1980

David G. Peterson, <u>The Acts of the Apostles</u>, Eerdmans, 2009

John Piper, <u>Why I Love the Apostle Paul</u>, Crossway, 2020

Eckhard J. Schnabel and Clinton Arnold, <u>Acts</u>, Zondervan, 2016

A Snapshot of Romans

Author

Paul, Apostle to the Gentiles

Date and Place of Writing

Romans was written from Corinth, near the end of Paul 's third missionary journey, AD 57. Tertius penned the letter for Paul (16:22) and Phoebe delivered it. (16:12). Paul had not been to Rome, but he had evidently met a number of the Roman Christians in his travels.

Recipients:

The believers in Rome. Rome was the cosmopolitan capital of the Roman Empire. The church in Rome would seem to have been composed of both Jews and Gentiles. There seems to have been several different congregations. (1) those who met at the home of Prisca and Aquila (16:3-5), (2) those associated with Asyncritus and others (16:14) and (3) those associated with Philologus (16:15).

Occasion of Writing

This letter was sent to prepare the church for Paul's anticipated visit to Rome (1: 10-15 and 15:22-24). The book reflects some underlying tensions between the Jewish and Gentile believers (15:5-7) fueled by some unnamed agitators (16:17-20) and disagreements over certain practices. (:1-15:13) Paul refers to Jews/Israel/Israelites 27 times and to Gentiles 28 times.

Purpose

1. To prepare the Roman church for his anticipated visit. [What Paul did not realize at the time that his

visit to Rome would be as a prisoner, though he did anticipate trouble in Jerusalem. (Acts 20:22-23, 25, 21:7-14)]

2. To lay out the basics of the Christian faith both in doctrine (1-11) and practice.

3. To put a stop to the potential Jew/Gentile division by showing that the gospel applied to both Jews and Gentiles alike.

Theme

The gospel is the power of God for salvation to Jews and Gentiles alike and reveals the righteousness of God. Key text: Romans 1:16-17

The Story

The New Testament Epistles do not necessarily contain much narrative. Paul only says that, as he was writing this, he was on his way to Jerusalem to deliver a love offering he had collected from the churches in Macedonia and Achaia. Then, he planned to come to Rome to visit them before going on to a mission to Spain. What he did not expect was that he would be arrested in Jerusalem, incarcerated in Caesarea for more than two years, sent to Rome for trial, and put under house arrest for another two years in Rome. We have no knowledge that he ever made it to Spain.

Outline

1. Introduction 1:1-17

2. Righteousness Needed: All people are guilty
    1:18-3:20

    1) The guilt of the Gentiles 1:18-32

    2) The guilt of the moralists. 2:1-16

    3) The guilt of the Jews.2:17-3:8

    4) The guilt of all people. 3:9-20

3. Righteousness Imputed: Justification by faith 3:21-5:21

1) The provision of righteousness manifested 3:21-26

2) The provision of righteousness harmonized with the Law 3:27-31

3) The provision of righteousness illustration 4:1-25

4) The provision of righteousness certified 5:1-24.

4. Righteousness imparted: Sanctification 6:1-8:39

   1) Its basis: Identification with the death and life

     of Christ 6:1-14

   2) Its principle: Enslavement to Christ 6:15-7:25

   3) Its power: The Holy Spirit 8:1-17

   4) Its future prospect 8:18-39

5. Righteousness vindicated 9:1-11:36

   1) In Israel's past: Election 9:1-29

   2) In Israel's present: Rejection 10:1-21

   3) In Israel's future: Restoration 11:1-36

6. Righteousness practiced 12:1-15:13

   1) In relationship with ourselves 12:1-2

   2) In relationship to ministry 12:3-8

3) In relationships to society 12:9-21

4) In relationship to government 13:1-14

5) In relationship to differences 14:1-15:13

    (1) The principle of liberty 14:1-12

    (2) The principle of love 14:13-33

    (3) The principle of unity 15:1-13

7. Epilogue

 1) Paul's plans 15:14-33

2) Personal greetings 16:1-16

3) Concluding admonition of benediction. 16:17-27

Characteristics and Points of Interest

1. Romans is the most complete presentation of the Gospel in the New Testament.

2. Romans 1:16-17 set forth the theme of this epistle.

3. One of the underlining concerns of Romans is the tension between Jewish and Gentile believers.

4. Romans includes profound theological truths including:

1) Salvation- Deliverance from the wrath of God. Deliverance from the penalty of sin. Righteousness imputed

2) Justification- God's declaration that the believing sinner is righteous.

3) Sanctification-Salvation from the power of sin as the believer appropriates power of the Holy Spirit to gain victory over indwelling sin. (Present) Righteousness practiced.

4) Glorification - Deliverance from the very presence pf sin. (Future) Righteousness perfected.

5) Redemption – that truth that by his death Jesus paid the penalty of our sins to free us from the consequences of sin. [3:24]

6) Reconciliation – the truth that the death of Jesus enables the believer to have peace with God, be brought back into harmony with God. [5:10]

7) Propitiation – the truth that the death of Jesus satisfied God's holy wrath against sin. [3:25]

8) The wrath of God: God's action in turning people over to their sin with its penalty and consequences. [1:18, 24, 26, 28, 5:9]

5. Romans stresses that salvation is obtained by faith in Jesus and not by keeping the Law or good works. [1:16-17, 3:20-26, 4:1-25, 5:1].

6. Romans contains strong teaching on the sovereignty of God in salvation.

 [Romans 8:28-30 9:6-24]

Major Applications

1. Romans is extremely important for understanding salvation.

2. Romans gives us important truth about how the truth of the Gospel should impact the ways we live. 12:1-2

3. Romans helps us understand how both Jews and Gentiles fit into God's plan.

Recommended Resources

F. F. Bruce, <u>The Epistles of Paul to the Romans</u>, Eerdmans

*F. F. Bruce, <u>Paul: Apostles of the Heart Set Free</u>, Eerdmans, 1977

John Harvey, <u>A Commentary on Romans</u>, Kregel, 2019

Colin G. Kruse, <u>Paul's Letter to the Romans</u>, Eerdmans, 2012

*Douglas Moo, <u>The Epistle to the Romans</u>, [NICNT] Eerdmans, 1996

A SNAPSHOT OF 1 CORINTHIANS

Author

Paul [1:1]

Date and Place of Writing

Betweeen AD 53-56 from Ephesus

Occasion

Paul had founded the church in Corinth on his second missionary journey. He was now in Ephesus on his third missionary trip and had heard reports about problems in the church [1:11, 5:1, 11:18] probably from Stephanas, Fortunatus and Achaicus [16:17] and had received questions they wanted him to answer [7:1].

Recipients

Church in Corinth. Corinth was the capital of the Roman province of Achaia. Corinth had a reputation as a city of wealth and immorality centered around the temple of Aphrodite and its thousands of temple prostitutes.

Purpose

To rebuke the Corinthian believers for divisions and disorderly conduct and to answer their questions about several practical and doctrinal matters. Part of his purpose was also to let them know his travel plans. [16:5-9]

Theme

The wise and mature Christian lives in unity, purity and love, following the authoritative words and example of the Apostle Paul.

The Story

During Paul extended stay in Ephesus on his third missionary journey Paul received reports about problems in the Corinthian church and received some questions they wanted answered. His information probably came from Stephanas, Fortunatus and Achaicus [16:17]. This letter addresses both of these issues. His plan was to leave Ephesus after Pentecost and travel through Macedonia to Corinth, where he intended to stay for the winter months. In the meantime, Timothy will be coming to Corinth. [16:5-11]

Outline:

1. Introduction 1:1-9

   1) Salutation 1:1-3

   2) Thanksgiving 1:4-9

2. The Problem of Divisions 1:10-4:2

   1) True Wisdom and the Foolishness of Divisions 1:10-2:16

      (1) The Foolishness of Divisions 1:10-17

      (2) An Excursus on Wisdom 1:18-2:15

   2) The Immaturity of Divisions 3:1-4

   3) A Discourse on Serving Christ 3:5-4:21

      (1) The Nature of Christian Service 5-17

      (2) The Proper Perspective on Service 3:18-4:5

      (3) Paul's Example of Service. 4:6-21

3. Problems for Discipline 5:1-6:20

   1) Incest 5:1-13

   2) Lawsuits 6:1-11

   3) Sexual Immorality 6:12-20

4. Issues for Discussion 7:1-16:4

   1) Marriage & Celibacy 7:1-40

   2) The Limits and Privileges of Christian Liberty. 8:1-11:1

      (1) The Principle of Deference to the Weaker Brother 8:1-13

      (2) Paul's Example of Self-limitation 9:1-27

(3) The Danger of Idolatry 10:1-22)

(4) Concluding Admonitions 10:23-11:1

3) Issues in the Public Assembly 11:2-14:40

(1) Women & Worship 11:2-16

(2) The Lord's Supper 11:17-34

(3) Spiritual Gifts 12:1-14:40

(4) The Doctrine of the Resurrection 15:1-58

5) The Collection 16:1-4

5. Concluding Words 16:5-24

Characteristics and Points of Interest

1. The authority of Paul as an Apostle is stressed by the directness of his commands [1:10, 5:3-5] the sharpness of his rebukes and warnings [1:13, 3:2-3, 16-17,4:6-10, 18-21,6:1,5, 11:17, 30, 14:12, 16:21-22], his claims to authority [1:1, 7:40, 11:1, 14:37-38] and commands to follow his example [4:16, 11:1,16]. He is an Apostle by the will of God [1:1].

2. The character issues of most concern in 1 Corinthians are: love: [8:1, 13:1-13, 16:1-2, 14,

24], unity [1:10, 3:1-9, 6:1-8, 11:17-19, 12:12-31, and sexual purity [5:1-13, 6:19-20, 7:1-5

3. Chapters 7-15 are unique in that they seem to be Paul's direct answers to some questions asked him in a letter from the Corinthians. Each new topic begins with the words "now concerning" except for chapter 15.

4. Corinth was notorious for its sexual immorality. "To Corinthianize" was a polite Greek way for saying "to practice immorality."

Major Applications

1. 1 Corinthians is a key book for the 21st century church. It guides the church in how to live wisely and maturely in a degenerate society. The problems plaguing the Church of Corinth: (1) lack of love, (2) disunity and (3) moral looseness also plague the 21st century church.

2. Chapter 15 is key teaching about the resurrection

3. Key texts for understanding such diverse topics as spiritual gifts, the church as a body, Christian liberty, marriage and singleness, and spirituality.

4. Assurance of salvation. Paul never once that they weren't saved in spite of their sinfulness.

Recommended Resources

D.A. Carson, Showing the Spirit: A Theological Exposition of 1Corinthians 12-14, Baker, 2019

*Gordon D. Fee, The First Epistle to the Corinthians Eerdmans, 1987

Paul D. Gardner and C. Arnold, 1 Corinthians, Zondervan, 2018

Thomas R. Schreiner, 1 Corinthians: An Introduction and Commentary, IVP, 2018

Gerd Theissen, The Social Setting of Pauline Christianity, Fortress, 2004

Anthony C. Thiselton, The First Epistles to the Corinthians [NIGTC] Eerdmans, 2000

Ben Witherington, <u>Conflict and Community in Corinth: A Socio-Rhetorical Commentary on 1 and 2 Corinthians</u> Eerdmans, 1995

Paul's Contacts with the Corinthians

1. Second missionary journey. Paul came to Corinth from Athens by himself.

He stayed with Aquila and Priscilla. He reasoned with the Jews in their synagogue.

Silas and Timothy came *to* him in Corinth. The ministry continued in the home of Titus Justus.

Paul was accused before Gallio. During this time he wrote the Thessalonian letters. AD 51-53

2. While Paul was in Ephesus [AD 53-55] he wrote a letter to the Corinthians.

It dealt in part with a matter of church discipline. They did not understand the letter correctly [1 Corinthians 5:9-13].

3. The family of Chloe visited Paul in Ephesus bringing news of disunity and other Problems [1 Corinthians 1:11]. Also, an official delegation from Corinth arrived bearing a gift for Paul from the church and a letter asking Paul about a series of written questions. [1 Cor. 7:1, 16:17]

In response Paul wrote 1 Corinthians to: (1) Acknowledge their gift, (2) clarify the matter of discipline, (3) address the problems shared by Chloe's people, (4) answer their questions, (5) announce his plans to visit them after Pentecost,

(6) prepare them to receive Timothy, and (7) encourage a collection for the believers in Jerusalem [1 Cor 4:14-19, 5:9 ,11, 7:1, 8:1, 12:1, 15:1, 16:1-12]

4. Paul made a visit to Corinth which is not recorded in Acts. It was a painful visit.

Its purpose was corrective. He was evidently not well-received by some in the church (some suggest he went himself because either Timothy was rejected or did not make it to Corinth). [1 Cor 4:18, 19, 2 Cor. 2:1, 12:14, 21]

5. After his return to Ephesus Paul wrote a third letter of warning and rebuke, evidently sending it with Titus [Some suggest that this is "severe" letter is preserved in 2 Corinthians 10-12]. The purpose of this letter was to arouse the church to deal with the rebels. [2 Cor 2:3, 4, 9, 7:8, 12]

6. Being very disturbed by the situation in Corinth, Paul left a potential ministry in Troas and went to Macedonia. There he met Titus who gave a generally good report of repentance and restoration, though problems remained related to agitation from some Judaizers who contested Pau's authority and apostleship. [2 Cor 2:12-13, Acts 20:1, 2 Cor 7: 5-7, 10:12, 11:4, 13, 22-23]

From Macedonia

Paul wrote 2 Corinthians to express his joy, to defend himself, his apostleship and his ministry, and to prepare them for his third visit. [2 Cor 7:5, 8:1, 9:2-4, 12:14, 13:10]

7. Paul probably did carry out his plans to visit them a third time.

He came from Macedonia and stayed three months before returning to Jerusalem via Macedonia, Troas, and Syria. It was probably from Corinth that Paul penned the book of Romans [Acts19: 21, 20:2-21:4, Rom. 15:23, 16:23]

A SNAPSHOT OF 2 CORINTHIANS

Author

Paul [1:1]

Date and Place of Writing

From Macedonia @ A.D. 56

Occasion

A verbal report from Titus as to the condition of the church. [2:12-13, 7:5-6, 13-16]

Purpose

To express his joy that there had been a reconciliation between him and the Corinthian church. [Chapters 1-7]

To explain to the church the change in his plans in respect to his visiting them

To refute the accusations of the false teachers,

To defend the authenticity of his apostleship,

To urge them to get their gift for the poor believers in Jerusalem ready to send. [Chapters 8-9]

To rebuke those who are repudiating his apostleship. [Chapters 10-13]

Theme

The nature of Paul 's Ministry: strength through weakness.

The Story

Paul had experienced trouble with the Corinthian church. After hearing negative reports from Chloe's household (1 Cor 1:11) and receiving further information from Stephanas, Fortunatus, and Achaicus (1 Cor. 16:17), Paul wrote 1 Corinthians to correct problems and to answer questions. The Corinthians had apparently not responded well to either 1 Corinthians or to a visit from Timothy. Therefore, Paul had made a visit to Corinth himself and had been insulted (2 Cor. 2:1).

He returned to Ephesus, where he wrote a strong letter of rebuke (2 Cor. 2:3-4, 9) and sent it with Titus. To this letter the Corinthians had responded rightly. The one(s) who had abused Paul repented. However, Paul became very anxious about the situation, wondering how they would respond to his letter. He left Ephesus and went to Troas. Still restless, Paul traveled across the Aegean Sea to Macedonia (north of Corinth) There in Macedonia Titus met him with a mixed report. One the one hand the offender(s) had repented, and the Corinthians were loyal to Paul and concerned about him. On the other hand, some false teachers had come into the church. They were trying to separate the Corinthian church from Paul and Paul 's message by accusing Paul of wrong motives and failure to really love the Corinthians. Therefore, Paul wrote 2 Corinthians from Macedonia.

One of the major efforts of Paul on his 2nd and 3rd missionary journeys was to collect an offering from the Gentile churches of Galatia, Asia, Macedonia and Achaia to give to the poor believers in the Jewish Jerusalem church.

The Corinthians had heard about this project and had written Paul about it. In 1 Corinthians 16:1-4 Paul directed them to begin to collect the gift. However, problems in Corinth between Paul and certain ones in the church had caused a delay in this collection. So, in 2 Corinthians 8 & 9 Paul writes to encourage them to complete the collection of this gift. The gift will be taken to Jerusalem by some delegates appointed by the churches (2 Cor 8:16-24; Acts 20:4) The offering was evidently collected (Rom 15:25-27) and then delivered (Acts 21:17).

Outline

3 obvious sections :

1-7 Look back-an explanation of his change of travel plans.

8-9 Present necessity to prepare for his coming.

10-13 Future-what he will do when he comes .

Introduction 1:1-11

1. Explanation of Paul's Ministry 1:12-7:16

   1) Paul explains his changed travel plans. 1:2-2:13

   2) Paul describes his Ministry. 2:14-7:16

     (1) Its character 2:14-3:6 (triumphant)

     (2) Its basis (the Spirit) 3:6-18

     (3) His conduct (power through trials) 4:1-5

     (4) His prospects 4:6-5:10

     (5) Its program 5:11-6:2

     (6) The marks of valid ministry 6:3-10

     (7) His appeal 6:11-7:16

2. Grace Giving 8:1-9:15

3. The Glory of the Ministry 10:1-13:10

   1) The privilege of approval 10:1-18

   2) The proof of his apostleship 11:1-12:18

   3) Final appeals 12:19-13:10

Conclusion 13:11-14

Characteristics

1. 2 Corinthians is one of Paul's most personal, emotional and intimate books. His tone is emotional: joy, warning, loving confrontation. He is baring his soul, "This is who I am and where I 'm coming from. You mean a lot to me, but those of you who are repudiating me are going to have to deal with me face to face."

2. The book seems to be built around an explanation of why he hadn't come to visit them as he planned 1:15-16 but with many digressions. 2:14-7:4 is a long excursus on the nature of Christian ministry.

3. Paul refers to some false teachers who have infiltrated the church, repudiating his ministry and apostleship, and questioning his motives. 5:12,

2 :17, 10:2, 10, 12, 11:12-15, 20, 22. They were probably Judaizers.

Major Applications

1. Principles of ministry.

2. Help in times of affliction, turmoil, weakness.

3. Relationships in the body of Christ.

Recommended Resources

Paul Barnet, The Second Epistle to the Corinthians, [NICNT] Eerdmans, 1997

*D. A. Carson, From Triumphalism to Maturity, Baker, 1984

George H. Guthrie, 2 Corinthians, Baker, 2015

Murray G. Harris, The Second Epistle to the Corinthians, Eerdmans, 2005

A SNAPSHOT OF GALATIANS

Author

Paul [1:1]

Date and Place of Writing

Written around AD 48 from Antioch and before the Jerusalem Council of Acts 15.

Recipients

The Galatian churches established by Paul and Barnabas on the first missionary journey as recorded in Acts 13-14. These churches were located in Antioch of Pisidia, Iconium, Lystra, and Derbe [4:14, Acts 14:11, 12, Gal 6:17, Acts 14:19]

Purpose

To demonstrate that salvation and spiritual living are by faith not by keeping the law.

Theme

Justification is by faith not by the works of the Law.

The Story

After Paul returned to Antioch [14:26-28] Judaizing teachers came to the churches in Galatia proclaiming that it was necessary to keep the Law in order to be justified (especially circumcision and keeping of Jewish holy days). The impetus for this teaching probably arose from a persecution of Jewish Christians by Jewish Zealots. These teachers, trying to impose the Law on the Galatian Christians, attempted to undermine the Gospel by disparaging Paul and casting doubts on his credentials as an Apostle.

Outline

1. Introduction. 1:1-10 (salutation and occasion)
2. The question of authority. (Paul's message and ministry is authentic) 1:11-2:21

3. The question of salvation (Paul's gospel is superior) 3:1-4:31

    1) A personal argument. 3:1-5,

    2) Scriptural evidence. 3:6-14,

    3) Logical proof 3:15-29,

    4) A historical argument. 4:1-11,

    5) A sentimental argument. 4:12-18,

    6) An allegorical argument. 4:19-31

4. The question of spiritual living 5:1-6:10

    1) The principle of liberty. 5:1-12

    2) The principle of love. 5:13-15

    3) The principle of walking by the Spirit. 5:16-26

    4) The principle of burden bearing. 6:1-5

    5) The principle of sharing. 6:6-10

5. Conclusion 6:11-18

Characteristics and Points of Interest

1. The tone of Galatians is sharp, blunt, urgent, argumentative, and frustrated.

In Galatians alone, Paul expresses no thanksgiving or praise for the recipients of his letter. [1:6, 3:1]

2. Galatians is one of four epistles in which Paul writes a personal greeting with his own hand. [6:11, 1 Cor. 16:21, Col. 4:18, 2 Thess. 3:17]. Usually, someone penned the letter for Paul. Only one is mentioned, Tertius in Romans 16:22

3. Galatians gives us the best indication of the nature of Paul's physical problem, evidently a problem with his eyes. [4:13-15, 6:11]

4. Galatians along with Romans are Paul's clearest teachings on salvation.

5. Paul's opponents in Galatia seem to be Judaizers who want to make keeping the Law, especially circumcision, a condition for salvation. [1:8-9, 2:4-6, 11-15, 3:1, 4:17, 5:10, 12, 18, 6:12-13]

6. Habakkuk 2:4 was a key verse in Paul's understanding of salvation. He quotes it in Romans 1:17 and Galatians 3:11

7. In Galatians Paul contrasts attempting to earn salvation by keeping the Law with salvation being provided by the atonement of Jesus received by faith.

8. It is somewhat difficult to determine how the history Paul gives in Galatians 1 & 2 fit with the account in Acts. I would suggest: (1) That Paul's stay in Arabia [Galatians 1:17] happened immediately after Acts 9:22. (2) That the trip to Jerusalem in Acts 9:26-29 is not mentioned in Galatians. (3) That Galatians1:21 follows Acts 9:30, (4) Then comes the year Paul and Barnabas spent ministering in Antioch [Acts 11:26], (5) a trip to Paul and Barnabas to Jerusalem bringing a gift for the needy believers in Jerusalem [Acts 11:29-30] which is the same visit Paul mentions in Galatians 2:1-10, (6) Paul's confrontation with Peter in Antioch [Galatians 2:11-14] (7) Then, the council in Jerusalem [Acts 15} which had not yet happened when Paul wrote Galatians.

9. It appears that Tychicus brought this letter to the Galatians. [6:21-22] Other possible letter-carriers include: 1 Corinthians-Timothy [1 Cor 16:22], Ephesians-Tychicus [Eph. 6:21-22], Philippians-Timothy and Epaphrodites [2:19, 25], Colossians-Tychicus and Onesimus [4:7-9], Philemon-Onesimus [12], Titus, Artemas or Tychicus [3:12].

Major Applications

1. Galatians clearly teaches us that salvation is by faith alone in Christ alone.

It is a good book to give us assurance and to present the Gospel to those who are tempted to think salvation can be earned by good works.

2. Galatians 5 is an important passage for Christian living.

3. Along with 1 Cor 16:1-4, 2 Corinthians 8 & 9, and 1 Timothy 6:3-19, Galatians 6:6-10 gives us important teaching on financial stewardship.

Recommended Resources

F. F. Bruce, <u>Commentary on Galatians</u>, Eerdmans, 1982

David A. deSilva, <u>Galatians</u>, [NICNT] Eerdmans, 2018

Ronald Y. K. Fung and F.F. Bruce, <u>The Epistle to the Galatians</u>, [2 Vols] [NICNT] Eerdmans, 1986, 1988

Mark S. Harman, <u>Galatians: Evangelical Biblical Theology Commentary</u>, Lexham 2021

*Douglas J. Moo, <u>Galatians</u>, [ECNT] Baker, 2013

Thomas R Schreiner and Clinton E. Arnold, <u>Galatians</u>, Zondervan, 2010

John Stott, <u>The Message of Galatians</u>, IVP, 2021

A SNAPSHOT OF EPHESIANS

Author

Paul [1:1]

Date and Place of Writing

Ephesians was written from Rome during Paul' s first Roman imprisonment. AD 60-62 [3:1-3] Ephesians was evidently written at the same time as Colossians and Philemon (and before Philippians) and carried to the Ephesian church by Tychicus. [6:2 1-22, Colossians 4:7-9, Philemon 12]

Recipients

Believers of the church of Ephesus (mostly Gentiles). [2:11, 3:1] The Ephesians letter was probably passed around to other churches. Some scholars believe it was a letter intended for several church based on the fact that the words "in

Ephesus" are omitted in several important Greek manuscripts

Purpose

To focus the attention of the believer on the nature and the responsibilities involved in our calling as the church, the body of Christ.

To exhort the Ephesians to live in a way consistent with their position in Christ.

Theme

In Christ-The exalted position and expected practice of His body, the church.

The Story

Ephesus was first visited by Paul on his second missionary journey [Acts 18:19-21]

He returned to Ephesus on his third journey and spent three years there evangelizing and teaching the church. Ephesus had become the capital of the

Roman province of Asia in 129 b.c. It became the center of Roman administration and headquarters of the Roman proconsul or governor. It was a free city of 200,000 to 300,000 people located on important east-west and north-south roads. And it had access to the sea. Its culture was a mix of Greek and Oriental traditions. The people were very superstitious. The center of Ephesian culture was the worship and temple of the goddess of fertility Artemis, whom the Romans worshipped as Dianna. The worship of this goddess was very crude, filled with many rituals, magic, and the use of temple prostitutes. Paul's stay in Ephesus was terminated by a riot inspired by a silversmith named Demetrius and some fellow tradesmen who profited from the pagan worship. [Acts 19:23-41] His concern about his relationship with the Corinthian church was also a part of his reasons for leaving [Acts 19:21-22, 1 Cor. 16:5-9, 2 Cor. 2:12,12:14-21, 13:1-10]. The Letter to the Ephesians was not occasioned any problems. It is not remedial, but preventative. Paul sent Tychicus with this letter to inform the Asian churches of his circumstances. At some point, probably after his release from house arrest in Rome, Paul directed Timothy to remain in Ephesus to continue the work [1 Tim. 1:3]

Outline

1. Our Exalted Position   1:1-3:21

   1) Greetings 1:1-2

   2) Our New destiny 1: -23

     (1) Chosen by the Father 1:3-6

     (2) Purchased by the Son 1:7-12

     (3) Sealed by the Spirit 1:13-14

     (4) A prayer for comprehension—new confidence 1:15-23

      a. The hope of our calling 1:18

      b. The glory of His inheritance 1:18

      c. The greatness of our power 1: 19-23

   3) Our new relationships 2:1-3:19

(1) We have a new lif e 2:1-10

(2) We have a new union 2: 11—22

(3) We have a new revelation—the mystery
3:2-13

(4) We need a new realization—prayer for
completion. 3:1, 14-19

   a. We need strength 3:14-17 a

   b. We need comprehension 3 17b-19a

   c. We need maturity 3:19b

   d. A doxology 3:20-21

2. Our Expected Practice 4:16, 6: 24

  1) An exhortation to walk worthy of our calling.
4:1

  2) The manner of a worthy walk 4 2 -6:9

    (1) Living in the body 4: 2-16

      a. Live in unity. 4:2-6

      b. Live in diversity. 4:7-16

    (2) Living in personal relationships 4:17-
6:9

      a. In newness. 4:17-234

      b. In love. 4:25-5:2

c. In light 5:3-14

d. In wisdom 5:15-20

e. In submission 5:21-6:9

    a) In marital life. 5:22-33

    b) In family life. 6:1-9

3) The means for living life worthy of our calling. 6:10-20

    (1) Taking up the armor of God. 6:10-17

    (2) Prayer 6:18-20

4. The Epilogue 6:21-24

Characteristics and Points of Interest

1. Ephesians is quite impersonal for a letter written to people with whom he had lived for three years. There is no personal greetings or mention of names other than that of the bearer of the letter.

2. Ephesians has a distinct two-part structure with 4:1 the divider between chapters 1-3 and 4-6.

3. Chapters 1-3 are primarily doctrinal in scope while 4-6 are practical ramifications of the doctrinal truth given in chapters 1-3.

4. Some of the key concepts in Ephesians are:

1) The believer's position "in Christ." "In Christ" or equivalent expressions [in him,

in the Beloved] are used 35 times in the book. [1:3, 4, 6, 7, 8]

2) The unity of the body (Jews and Gentiles) 1:12-13 we—you 2:11-32, 3:6, 4:3-6, 11-16, 25, 4:31-5:1

3) Love—word root used 19 times,

4) Walk [4:1, 17, 5:2, 8, 15]

5. Ephesians 2 is one of the clearest teachings in the Bible on salvation

Major Applications

1. Ephesians helps us understand the nature of the Church, the body of Christ.

2. Ephesians shows us how we ought to live out our faith.

3. Ephesians shows the relationship between doctrine and living.

4. Ephesians has the most extensive N.T. teaching on the family. 5:22-6:9

5. Ephesians 2:1-10 is a great evangelistic text.

Recommended Resources

*Harold W. Hoehner, Ephesians: An Exegetical Commentary, Baker, 2002

John MacArthur, Ephesians, Moody, 1986

Peter T. O'Brian, The Letter to the Ephesians Eerdmans, 1999

J. Armitage Robinson, Commentary on Ephesians, Kregel, 1979

John Stott, God' s New Society: The Message of Ephesians, IVP, 1980

Warren W. Wiersbe, Be Rich, Victor, 2009

A Snapshot of Philippians

Author

 Paul [1:1]

Date and Place of Writing

Rome AD. 62. Paul is expecting acquittal, but he is not completely sure yet. [1:19,25; 2:17,23,24]

Recipients

The Philippian Church, and its leaders. [1:1]

Purpose

Philippians has no one purpose. Several can be cited:

1. To thank (commend) them for their financial gift. [4:10-19]

2. To express his love for them [1:7-8, 4:1]

3. To inform them of his situation and plans. [1:12-26, 2:19,23-24]

4. To exhort them regarding certain problems in their church.

1) Disunity [1:27, 2:24, 4:2]

2) Judaizers [3:2-19]

3) Temptation to desert. (because of opposition) [1:27-28, 4:1]

4) The need for joy irrespective of circumstances. [2:18, 3: 1, 4:4]

Theme

Some believe the theme of Philippians is *joy* (used 16 times in the book). I would suggest *Living a godly life.* See 1:27.

The Story

Paul, Silas, Luke and Timothy first visited Philippi on his second missionary journey in response to a divine vision. Some were saved including Lydia and a jailer and a church was established, but his stay was not long. [Acts 16].

After Paul left the believers sent him financial gifts at least twice [Phil 4:16, 2 Cor. 11:9] Luke evidently stayed on in Philippi until Paul returned there at the end of his third journey and then accompanied Paul to Jerusalem. Near the end his third missionary journey Paul evidently passed through Philippi twice and left for Jerusalem from Philippi. [Acts 19:21-22, 20:1-6, 2 Cor 2:13] The Macedonian churches, probably including Philippi, sent a gift with Paul for the needy believers in Judea. The Philippian church representative may have been a man named Gaius [Acts 19:29]

While Paul was in prison in Rome the Philippians sent Epaphroditus to Rome with a financial gift for him. [4:18] He stayed with Paul, got critically ill, recovered, then returned to Philippi, evidently carrying this letter. [2:25-30] Paul also intended to send Timothy to minister to them. [2:19-24] And he wrote that he felt confident that he was going to be released from prison, and if so, he planned to revisit them. [1:25, 2:24]

It seems likely that that did happen [1 Tim. 1:23]

Characteristics and Points of Interest

1. Philippians is a very personal and practical letter.

2. It is warm, cordial, joyful and hopeful.

3. It is not devoid of doctrine. Christ's incarnation and exaltation [2:5-11] and the return of Christ [3:20-21]. But its emphasis is on practical Christian living.

4. Some sub-themes: fellowship, participation in and with Christ, The Gospel, attitudes.

5. The false teachers are Judaizers, Christian Jews who taught circumcision and perfectionism.

Outline:

1. Encouragement for living a godly Christian Life

1: 1-30

1) Praise 1:1-8

2) Prayer 1:9-11

3) Present Circumstances 1:12-26

4) Prescription 1:27-30

2. Examples of godly Christian living 2:1-30

   1) Exhortation to unity and humility 2:1-4

   2) Example of Christ 2:5-11

   3) Paul 2:12-18

   4) Timothy 2:19-24

   5) Epaphroditus 2:25-30

3. Exhortation for living a godly life. 3:1-4:9

   1) Warning against false teachers 3:1-20

   2) Other exhortations 4:1-9

4. Epilogue 4:10-23

   1) Expressing gratitude for their gift 4: 10-20

   2) Final greetings 4:21-23

Major Applications

1.   For understanding the doctrine of Christ's incarnation. [2:1-11]

2.   The possibility of joy in adversity. [1:18, 4:4]

3.   The blessings of the fellowship of the saints. [1:3-11, 2:19-30]

4.   A proper view of material things. [4:10-19]

5. A proper perspective on life and death. [1:20-24]

6. Teaching in respect to the mind/thoughts/attitudes. [2:1-5, 4:4, 8-9]

7. The importance of unity. [1:27, 2:2-4, 14]

8. The goal of Christian living. [3:8-16]

9. Expressing love, joy, gratitude, giving a good report [2:19-30]

Recommended Resources

*Gordon D. Fee, Paul's Letter to the Philippians [NICNT] Eerdmans, `1995

G. Walter Hansen, The Letter to the Philippians, Eerdmans, 2009

William Hendricksen, Philippians, Colossians and Philemon, Baker, 1962

John MacArthur, Philippians: The Source of Joy and Strength, Moody, 2015

H. C. G. Moule, Philippian Studies, Pickering & Inglis. n.d.

Peter T. O'brien, The Letter to the Philippians, NIGTC] Eerdmans, 1991

Grant R. Osborne, <u>Philippians Verse by Verse</u>, Lexham, 2017

Moises Silva, <u>Philippians</u>, Baker, 2005

A SNAPSHOT OF COLOSSIANS

Author

Paul [1:1, 23, 4:18]

Date and Place of Writing

AD 60-62 From a prison in Rome. [4:10, 12, 18 cf. Philemon 1, 9, 22, 23]

Recipients

To the church at Colossae. Colossae was decaying town in the Lycus valley about 100 miles east of Ephesus. Colossae was overshadowed by its two prosperous neighbors, 12 miles to the west, Laodicea and Hierapolis. All were destroyed by an earthquake a few years later. The church may have grown out of Paul's Ephesian ministry [3rd missionary journey] [Acts 19:10], but Paul had not been there personally [2:1]. Epaphras had evangelized these three cities [1:7, 4:13]. It was a mostly Gentile church 1:27, 4:13

Theme

Jesus Christ is supreme: We live and walk in him.

Purpose

1. To present the truth and implications of our union with Christ, who is fully God.

2. To counteract a particular heresy in the Colossian church. The Colossian heresy was a syncretic belief containing elements of Judaism, the native Colossian paganism, and a Greek religious philosophy which eventually developed into Gnosticism.

1) Ritualistic element, especially Jewish—related

 rituals [2:16-17]

2) Ascetic element—depriving the body—

 concept that the body is evil. [2:18,20-23]

3) Mystical element—worship of angels and

demons. [2:18]

4) A denial or diminishing of the centrality of divine nature of Christ. [2:8-9,19]

5) Dependence on the intellect. "super knowledge"

3. To lead them past or out of this heresy to maturity in Christ. [1:28, 2:6-7]

4. To inform them as to the mission of Tychicus. [4:7-9]

The Story

The Colossian church may have grown out of Paul's Ephesian ministry [3rd missionary journey] [Acts 19:10], but Paul had not been there personally [2:1]. Epaphras, who was from Colossae, had evangelized these three cities [1:7, 4:12-13]. The occasion for the writing of this letter was the returning of the slave Onesimus to his master Philemon—both members of the Colossian church [Philemon]. It appears that Tychicus delivered the letter to them. [Col 4:7-9] along with the letter to the Ephesians and the letter to Philemon. We have no information as to whether [Ephesians 6:21] Paul himself ever visited Colossae.

Outline

Prologue 1:1-2

1. The Person of Jesus Christ 1:3-2:5

    1) Paul's prayer 1:3-14, Thanksgiving 3-8 Intercession 9-14.

    2) Christ the Preeminent One 1:15-23. In creation 15-17 and in the church 18-23

    3) Proclamation of Christ 1:25- 2:5

2. The practice of life in Christ 2: 623

    1) Basic Principles 6-15

    2) Implications for Living 16-23

3. Perspectives in living life in Christ 3:1-4:4

    1) The mind-set 3:1-4

    2) Personal responsibilities 5-17

    3) Relational responsibilities 3:18-4:6

Epilogue 4:17-18

Characteristics and Points of Interest

1. Similarity in thought with Ephesians in the practical portion.

2. The centrality of Christ and the "In Christ relationship".

3. Tone—firm but friendly.

4. Like Ephesians, Colossians has two distinct sections a doctrinal section [1-2]

   followed by a practical section [3-4].

Major Applications

1. To focus our attention on Christ.

2. For those faltering in their Christian life due to inadequate understanding as to

   the centrality of Christ.

3. To those in danger of falling into legalism.

Recommended Resources

William Hendricksen, <u>Philippians, Colossians and Philemon</u>, Baker, 1962

Scott McKnight, <u>The Letter to the Colossians,</u> [NICNT] Eerdmans, 2018

*Douglas J. Moo, <u>The Letters to the Colossians and to Philemon</u>, Eerdmans, 2008

H. C. G. Moule, <u>Colossians and Philemon Studies</u>, Pickering & Inglis, 1981

Peter T. O'brien, <u>The Letters to the Colossians and Philemon</u>, Word, 1982

David W. Pao and Clinton E. Arnold, <u>Colossians and Philemon</u>, [ECNT] Zondervan, 2012

A Snapshot of 1 Thessalonians

Author

Paul the Apostle [1:1]

Date & place of writing

From Corinth in AD 50 on his second missionary journey. Chronologically this is the second of Paul's preserved letters.

Recipients

The church of Thessalonica which was the chief seaport of the Roman province of Macedonia with an estimated population of 200,000. It was populated by Greeks, Romans and Jews. It had the status of a free governing city. The Roman governor resided there.

Purpose:

1. To commend them for their response to the gospel amid opposition.

2. To defend his ministry among them which was probably being defamed by certain Jews who were saying that Paul was a charlatan who cared nothing about them except for their money.

3. To instruct them, especially concerning the return of Christ.

4. To urge them to live godly lives.

Theme: Faith (past), love (present), and hope (future). Key verses: 1 :3, 5:8.

The Story

These Thessalonians had come to Christ during Paul's second missionary journey with Silas and Timothy. (Acts 17: 1-9) From Thessalonica the missionaries turned to Berea. From Berea Paul sent Timothy back to Thessalonica (3:1, 2, 5). Silas stayed in Berea and Paul went on to Athens (Acts 17:13-15). At Athens Paul sent for the two (Acts 17:15). They caught up with him in Corinth (Acts 18:5). Timothy then gave Paul a report about the Thessalonians. This report inspired Paul to write 1 Thessalonians.

Outline

1. Introduction 1:1-10

    1) Salutation V. 1

    2) Rendering thanks V. 2-3

    3) Recounting faith. V. 4-10

2. The work connected to faith. 2:1-3 : 1

    1) Paul's past work in bringing them the gospel.

      V. 1-12

    2) Their demonstration of faith. V. 13-16

3) Paul's present concern for them. V. 2:17-3:10

3. The labor inspired by love. 4:1-12

   1) The hard work of sexual purity. V. 1-8

   2) The hard work of loving each other. V. 9-10

   3) The hard work of work. V. 11-12

4. The steadfastness inspired by hope. 4:13-5:22

   1) Waiting for departure (The Rapture) 4:13-

     18

   2) Waiting for deliverance (Day of the Lord) 5:1-

     11

   3) The way to live while waiting. 5:12-22

5. Final words. 5:23-28

Characteristics

1. 1 Thessalonians has a warm tone.

2. Some scholars see a chiastic structure in the book (abcddcba).

3. The letter contains one of clearest New Testament texts on the Rapture.

   (1:10, 4:13-18, 5:1-9)

4. I believe 1:3 gives us the progression of Paul's thoughts in the letter.

Major Applications

1. That we would find assurance in our journey of faith.

2. That we would develop faith, hope and love.

3. That we would have a clearer understanding of the future.

Recommended Resources

F. F Bruce, 1 & 2 Thessalonians Word, 1982

*Gordon Fee, The First and Second Letters to the Thessalonians [NICNT] Eerdmans. 2009

Gene L. Green, The Letters to the Thessalonians, Eerdmans, 2002

Abraham Malherbe, <u>Paul and The Thessalonians</u>, Fortress, 1987

Gant R. Osborne, <u>1 & 2 Thessalonians Verse by Verse</u>, Lexham, 2018

Gary Shogren and Clinton E. Arnold, <u>1 & 2 Thessalonians</u>, Zondervan, 2012

Charles Wanamaker, <u>The Epistles to the Thessalonians</u> [NIGNT] Eerdmans, 1990

Jeffery A. D. Weima and Robert Yarbrough, <u>1 & 2 Thessalonians</u>, Eerdmans, 2014

A Snapshot of 2 Thessalonians

Author

Paul [1:1]

Date and Place of Writing

From Corinth, on his second missionary journey @ A.D. 50, 51

Recipients

The Thessalonian believers [1:1]

Purpose

1. To commend the church for their enlarged faith, growing love, and steadfast endurance in the midst of suffering.

2. To correct some doctrinal and practical errors relating to the coming of Christ.

Theme

Assurance of the Lord's return gives the believer comfort and strength.

The Story

These Thessalonians had come to Christ during Paul's second missionary journey with Silas and Timothy. (Acts 17: 1-9) From Thessalonica the missionaries turned to Berea. From Berea Paul sent Timothy back to Thessalonica (3: 1, 2, 5). Silas stayed in Berea and Paul went on to Athens (Acts 17:13-15). At Athens Paul sent for the two (Acts 17:15). They caught up with him in Corinth (Acts 18:5). Timothy then gave Paul a report about the Thessalonians. This report inspired Paul to write 1 Thessalonians. Subsequently, some false teachers, perhaps even forging Paul's signature to their teachings [2:2], were teaching that the Day of the Lord had begun. If these were Judaizers, they were perhaps suggesting that the believers' suffering and persecutions were judgment from God associated with the prophetic judgments of the Day of the Lord. So, Paul writes again perhaps just a few months after his first letter to them.

Outline

Prologue 1:1-2

1. Introduction 1:11-12

   1) Thanksgiving 1: 3-4 (faith, love, and steadfast

     endurance.)

   2) Assurances 1:5-10

     (1) Their suffering will be rewarded .

     (2) Their persecutors will be punished. 1: 6-
       10

   3) Prayer. 1:11-12

2. Instructions in Right Doctrine 2:1-17

1) The true doctrine of Christ's coming 2:1-12

    (1) Wrong teaching 2:1-2 [The Day of the Lord has come]

    (2) Refutation of the wrong reaching 2:3-12

        a. The apostasy must come first. 3a

        b. The Man of Sin must be revealed. 3b-12

2) The true doctrine of our calling 2:13-14

    (1) The plan of salvation. 2:13

    (2) The purpose of salvation 2:14

    (3) Deductions for our living 2:15

        a. Steadfastness in doctrine

        b. Stability in deportment

3) Prayer 2:16-17

3. Injunctions for Right Living 3:1-16

    1) A call to prayer and confidence 3:1-5

        (1) Plea for prayer 3:1-2

        (2) A Profession of assurance 3:3-5

    2) Commands concerning correcting errant practice 3:6-15

(1) The commands stated 6

(2) The principle illustrated 7-10

(3) The commands expanded 11-15

3) Prayer 3:16

Epilogue 3:17-18

Characteristics and Points of Interest

1. The tone of this book is warm and thankful.

2. This book is both instruction and exhortation.

3. Chapter two gives teaching respect to the return of Jesus.

4. Chapter three gives instruction about a matter for church discipline.

Major Applications

1. Wrong doctrine (the Day of the Lord has come) produces wrong living (loss of hope and careless living). Right doctrine should lead to right living. Doctrine does make a difference.

2. The practical importance of the study of the last things (Eschatology). The loss of hope leads to carelessness, a lack of commitment and apathy.

3. The need to pray for one another.

4. The need for balance in ministry: Praise, thanksgiving, intercession, exhortation, doctrinal instruction: all are needed.

5. Church discipline is taught in this book.

Recommended Resources:

F. F Bruce, 1 & 2 Thessalonians Word, 1982

*Gordon Fee, The First and Second Letters to the Thessalonians [NICNT] Eerdmans. 2009

Gene L. Green, The Letters to the Thessalonians, Eerdmans, 2002

Abraham Malherbe, Paul and The Thessalonians, Fortress, 1987

Gant R. Osborne, 1 & 2 Thessalonians Verse by Verse, Lexham, 2018

Gary Shogren and Clinton E. Arnold, 1 & 2 Thessalonians, Zondervan, 2012

Charles Wanamaker, The Epistles to the Thessalonians [NIGNT] Eerdmans, 1990

Jeffery A. D. Weima and Robert Yarbrough, 1 & 2 Thessalonians, Eerdmans, 2014

Warren W. Wiersbe, Be Ready Victor. 2010

A SNAPSHOT OF TIMOTHY

Timothy was probably a native of Lystra (or Derbe) in the Roman Province of Galatia. Lystra consisted of native Lyconian people as well as Greeks, Jews and Romans. Timothy's father was a Greek and evidently not a believer and his mother Eunice was Jewish. [Acts 16:1]. Timothy had been faithfully taught the Scriptures from early childhood. [2 Timothy 3:15] First, Timothy's mother Eunice and his grandmother Lois had become Christians and then Timothy. [2 Timothy 1:5] Timothy's conversion may have happened when Paul had come to the area on his first missionary journey [AD 49-50]. Paul may have led Timothy to Christ as he calls him his son [Philippians 2:22].

When Paul returned to Lystra and Derbe on his second missionary journey [AD 50-52], he decided to take Timothy along with him because Timothy was well-spoken of by the churches in Lystra and Iconium. Paul had Timothy circumcised so as not to offend the Jews [Acts 16:1-3]. Sometime during this time Timothy had received gifting for ministry through the laying on of hands by the elders and Paul. [2 Timothy 1:6, 4:14]. Paul's reference to Timothy's having "made the good confession in the presence of many witnesses" in 1 Tim 6:12 may refer to his baptism. When Paul left Berea for Athens, Silas and Timothy remained behind in Berea. [Acts 16:14-15], though Timothys seems to be in Athens when

Paul sent him back to Thessalonica to see how the new believers there were doing and continue to establish them in the truth. He then joined up with Paul again in Corinth giving a good report of the work in Thessalonica. [Acts 18:5, 2 Corinthians 1:19, 1 Thessalonians 1:1, 3:1-6, 2 Thessalonians 1:1]. He may have been one of those who had brought a financial gift to Paul when Paul was in Corinth [2 Corinthians 11:9], perhaps from the Philippians [Philippians 4:15].

Timothy was with Paul on at least on part of Paul's third missionary journey, particularly in Ephesus [Acts 19:22]. Timothy was sent to Corinth by Paul to deal with problems in the church of Corinth, a mission which probably did not turn out well. [1 Corinthians 4:17, 16:10-11] since Paul then sent Titus to Corinth. While awaiting Titus' return Paul became anxious and went to Troas [2 Corinthians 2:12] and then to Macedonia where Titus came to Paul with an encouraging report [2 Corinthians 7:5-7].

Timothy was with Paul in Macedonia at the time of the writing of 2 Corinthians [2 Corinthians 1:1]. He was with Paul in Corinth when Paul wrote his letter to the Romans [Romans 16:21). Timothy was one of those who traveled with Paul to Jerusalem when Paul was arrested and imprisoned. [Acts 20:4]

He was with Paul at least part of the time of Paul's first Roman imprisonment [AD 60-62]. [Colossians 1:1, Philippians 1:1] Paul informed the Philippians that he was planning to send Timothy to them [Philippians 2:19].

Sometime after Paul was released from prison, he left Timothy in Ephesus to oversee the church. When Paul was imprisoned in Rome a second time [@AD 65], evidently Timothy was still in Ephesus. In his second letter to Timothy, Paul asked Timothy to come to him in Rome with Mark stopping in Troas to bring Paul some books and parchments [2 Timothy 4:9-11, 21]. He evidently had some digestive troubles [1 Timothy 5:23].

Hebrews 13:23 suggests that Timothy himself was in prison for a time.

As to Timothy's character we have the testimony of Luke [in Acts], Paul, and the author of Hebrews. According to Luke he had a good reputation in Lystra and Iconium. Paul called him his brother [2 Corinthians 1:1], God's coworker in the gospel [1 Thessalonians. 3:2], a fellow worker [Rom 16:21], "my beloved and faithful child in the Lord." [1 Cor. 4:17, 1 Timothy 1:2], and a man of God [1 Timothy 6:11]. Paul commends Timothy as one who was genuinely concerned for others, of proven worth, a faithful servant [Phil 2:19-22], and a man of sincere faith [2 Timothy 1:5]. He remarked on Timothy's tearful love for himself [2 Timothy 1:4]. 1 Corinthians 16:10-11 and 2 Timothy 1:6-7 may suggest that he may have been timid, but the responsibilities Paul entrusted him with (e.g. confronting false teaching) speak otherwise.

A SNAPSHOT OF 1 TIMOTHY

Author

Paul [1:1]

Date and Place of writing

@AD 63-66; probably from Macedonia [1:3] Probably after Paul's release from prison and before he was imprisoned a second time in Rome.

Recipient

Timothy, a protege of Paul, whom Paul met on his second missionary journey ([Acts 16:1), had accompanied Paul on his second and third missionary journeys and to Rome.

After his release from prison in Rome Paul visited Asia and dropped Timothy off to lead the Ephesian church [1Timothy 1:3]. Timothy and Titus were not strictly pastors as we think of pastors but Paul's personal apostolic representatives.

Purpose

To explain to Timothy how the church is to function, and how he is to function in the church. [3:14-16]

To instruct Timothy to stop the false teachers. [1:3-7, 18-20, 4:1-8, 6:3-10, 20]

Theme

The church and those who lead it must function so as to promote and display godliness and sound doctrine. On godliness: [1 Timothy 2:2,10, 3:16, 4:7-8, 5: 4, 6:3-6, 11]. On sound teaching [1:10, 4:6,13,16, 6:1-3].

The Story

Upon his release from prison in Rome Paul traveled various places and left Timothy in Ephesus to lead the church and deal with false teachers who had arisen from within the church leadership in Ephesus. When Paul was re-incarcerated in Rome he sent for Timothy, replacing him in Ephesus with Tychicus. [2 Timothy 4:9-12]

Outline:

Salutation 1:1-2

1. Public Responsibilities in the Household of God 1:3-3:13

   1) Of Timothy 1:3-20

   2) Of men 2: 1-8

   3) Of women 2:9-15

   4) Of leaders 3: 1-13 [Elders 3: 1-7, Deacons 3: 8-13)

2. The Theme Presented 3:14-16

3. Personal Relationships the Household of God 4:1-6:1

   1) With various groups of people 4:1-6:2

      (1) Relationships with false teachers and

false teaching 4:1-10

    (2) Relationships with the congregation 4:11-16

    (3) Relationships with men 5:1

    (4) Relationships with women 5:2

    (5) Relationships with widows 5:3-16

    (6) Relationships with rulers 5:17-6:2

  2) In relation to things 6:3-19

Conclusion 6:20-21

Characteristics and Points of Interest

1. 1 Timothy is personal, practical, fatherly, emotional and exhortative.

2. 1 Timothy gives us the most specific information about leadership in the local church. Qualifications for elders and deacons are listed in 3:1-13

3. Evidently false teaching had entered the church. From Paul's comments it appears to have included legalistic elements including asceticism, allegorical interpretation of the Old Testament,

aspects of paganism, and pre-Gnostic philosophy (secret knowledge). [1:3-4, 6-7, 19-20, 4:1-3, 7, 6:3-5, 20-21]

4. Bible students have recognized Paul's "faithful" or "trustworthy" sayings

[1 Timothy 1:15, 3:1, 4:9, 2 Timothy 2:11, and Titus 3:8]

5. 1 Timothy 2:15 is one of the most difficult verses in 1 Timothy to understand.

My take on this verse is that, though certain aspects of public ministry by women in the church are restricted, yet a woman with godly children would have a voice in the assembly (saved from having no voice) through their children. Others see "childbearing" as a reference to the birth of Jesus and "saved" as a reference to receiving eternal life.

6. 1 Timothy 6:5-10, 17-19 are important teachings on money.

Major Applications

1. 1Timothy is a great resource for ordering the life of a church.

2. 1 Timothy is a great resource for church leaders.

3. 1 Timothy encourages the development of godliness.

4. 1 Timothy reminds us of the danger of false teaching infiltrating the church.

5. The teaching in 6:3-10-17-19 is helpful for our financial management.

Recommended Resources

George W. Knight, Commentary on the Pastoral Epistles, [NICGT] Eerdmans

George W. Knight III, The Faithful Sayings in the Pastoral Letters, Baker, 1979

George W. Knight III, The Pastoral Epistles, Eerdmans, 1992

J. N. D. Kelly, The Pastoral Epistles: I & II Timothy, Titus, Adam & Charles Black, 1963

*Abraham Kuruvilla, 1 & 2 Timothy and Titus, Eerdmans

H. P. Liddon, Explanatory Analysis of St. Paul's First Epistle to Timothy, Klock & Klock, 1978 Reprint of original publication by Longmans, Green & Co, 1897

John F. MacArthur, 1 Timothy: Encouragement for Church Leaders, Moody, 2016

Philip H. Towner, The Letters to Timothy, Titus [NICNT] Eerdmans, 2006

David C. Verner, The Household of God: The Social World of the Pastoral Epistles, Scholars Press, 1983

Warren Wiersbe, Be Faithful, Victor Books, 2009

A Snapshot of 2 Timothy

Author

Paul [1:1]

Recipient

Timothy (probably still at Ephesus. [2 Timothy 4:12, 14, 15, 1 Timothy 1:21, 2 Timothy 1:16-18, 4:19]

Date and Place of Writing

@67 shortly before Paul's martyrdom in Rome.

Purpose

1. To encourage Timothy to remain faithful to the Lord, to the truth and to his ministry.
2. To request that Timothy come to Rome to visit him before winter arrived.
[4:9-13, 21]

Theme

Faithfulness in serving the Lord in the face of hardship.

The Story

After Paul had been re-incarcerated in Rome and was aware that the end of his life was coming soon, he wrote Timothy to ask him to come to Rome with Mark for one last visit. [2 Timothy 4:9-12] We can only assume that this happened. It seems that Tychicus was probably the letter carrier [4:12]

Outline:

Salutation 1:1-2

1. Exhortation to faithfulness expounded 1:3-18

    1) Paul's concern for Timothy 1:3-5

    2) His exhortation to Timothy 1:6-14

    3) His exhortation illustrated 1:15-18

2. Exhortation to faithfulness expanded 2:1-4:8

    1) General principles. 2:1-3

(1) The principles in summary. v. 1-2

What needs to be done to maintain faithfulness

(2) The principles in particular.

    a. Suffer hardship 2:3-7

    b. Remember 2:8-13

        a) Remember examples 2:8-10 [of Christ, of

        Paul]

        b) Remember the promises 2:11-13

2) Specific procedures to enhance faithfulness. 2:14 - 3:17

    Seven imperatives/responsibilities for Timothy

    (1) Remind 2:14

    (2) Be diligent 2:15

    (3) Avoid false teaching 2:16-21

    (4) Flee youthful lusts. 2:22

    (5) Refuse the engage in fruitless arguments. 2:23-26

    (6) Realize the nature of the times. 3:1-9

        a. Summary 3:1

b. The character of the ungodly. 3:2-5 [19 negative traits]

c. The conduct of the ungodly false teachers. 3:6-8

d. The coming end of the ungodly. 3:9

(7) Continue in the truth. 3:10-17

There is an obvious contrast between the ungodly and the false teachers on the one hand and Paul and Timothy on the other.

a. Timothy's past responsiveness in following Paul's example. 3:10-13 Nine virtues

b. Timothy's present responsibility. 3:14-17

Timothy is urged to continue in the truth and in godliness on the basis of the several realities.

a) The reliability of his teachers. 3:14

b) The reliability of what he was taught (the Scriptures) 3: 15-17

(a) The Scriptures are the source of wisdom and salvation. 3:15

(b) The Scriptures are from God. 3:16

(c)The Scriptures are profitable. 3:17

3) Particular Tasks. 4:1-8

3. Epilogue 4:9-22

Characteristics & Points of Interest

1. 2 Timothy is warm, personal, fatherly, emotional, and exhortative.

2. These are the words of a wise godly older man at the end of his life.

3. 2 Timothy has an eschatological emphasis. [1:1, 12, 18, 2:12, 3:1, 4:1,6-8,18]

4. 2 Timothy 3:16-17 are key verses on the inspiration of Scripture.

5. 2 Timothy 2:2 is a key verse on discipleship.

Major Applications

Encouragement for believers as servants of God. Encouragement for those engaged in spiritual ministry. 2 Timothy is good book for devotionals to share with camp counselors, S. S. teachers,

VBS workers, and church committees. Encouragement for those facing opposition or tempted to quit serving the Lord.

A good book to preach at the end of a pastoral ministry.

Recommended Resources

J.N.D. Kelly, The Pastoral Epistles: I & II Timothy, Titus, A & C Black, 1963

George W. Knight II, The Faithful Sayings in the Pastoral Letters, Baker, 1979

*George W. Knight III, Commentary on The Pastoral Epistles, [NICGT], Eerdmans, 1992

Abraham Kuruvilla, 1 & 2 Timothy and Titus: A Theological Commentary for Preachers, Cascade, 2021

John F. MacArthur, 1 Timothy: Encouragement for Church Leaders, Moody, 2016

John Stott, Guard the Gospel: The Message of 2 Timothy, IVP, 2021

Philip Towner, The Letters to Timothy, Titus [NICNT] Eerdmans

Warren Wiersbe, Be Faithful, Victor Books, 2009

Philip H. Towner, The Letters to Timothy, Titus [NICNT] Eerdmans, 2006

David C. Verner, The Household of God: The Social World of the Pastoral Epistles, Scholars Press, 1983

A SNAPSHOT OF TITUS

Author

Paul [1:4]

Recipient

Titus, a Greek believer and companion of Paul. [Galatians 2:1]

He ministered in Corinth [2 Corinthians 2:13; 8:16, 23]

Date and place of writing

(AD 62-66) between Paul's imprisonments.

Purpose

1. To encourage Titus to finish the task of setting the church in order so it functions properly.

2. To encourage Titus to teach a sound pattern for family life.

3. To encourage Titus to teach believers a godly perspective for living in this world and relating to the world and its people.

4. To ask Titus to meet him in Nicopolis.

Theme:

Living a godly life, which is rich in good works. [1:1, 2:12, 3:1,8,14]

The Story

Titus was evidently a Gentile believer [Gal. 2:3]. It may be that Paul had led him to Christ. [Titus 1:4]. He became one of Paul's ministry associates whom Paul greatly appreciated and respected [2 Cor. 8:23].

The first historical reference to Titus comes when he traveled with Paul to Jerusalem. [Gal. 2:1-10] This was probably the trip Paul and Barnabas made to take a gift to the needy believers in Jerusalem [Acts 11:25-30] @ AD 46 or 47. During the same trip Paul met privately with the leaders of the Jerusalem church and apostles (Paul calls them "those who seemed influential") to inform them of his ministry among the Gentiles and the message he preached. They accepted both his message and his mission to the Gentiles. However, there seems to have been some pressure on Titus to be circumcised, but Paul would not yield to that demand.

The next we hear about Titus is in Paul second letter to the Corinthians written from Macedonia on Paul's third missionary journey [A.D. 55-56] Paul had sent Titus and another unnamed brother to Corinth evidently to resolve a problem that had arisen between Paul and the Corinthians and to complete the collection of a love offering for the Jerusalem believers [2 Cor. 8:6,18-19]. He had sent Titus because he knew Titus had the same heart for the Corinthians as he himself had [2 Cor. 8:16-17]. Titus may have carried with him a "harsh letter" [which we do not have] from Paul concerning about affairs in Corinth. [2 Cor 2:3-4, 7:8]

Paul had left Ephesus and expected to meet Titus in Troas. Not finding Titus in Troas Paul had traveled on into Macedonia. [2 Cor 2:13]. Titus did connect with Paul in Macedonia and was able to give him an encouraging report about the Corinthians' love for Paul. Titus had left Corinth encouraged by the time he had spent there. [2 Corinthians 7:6-9, 13] Like Paul, Titus had not taken financial advantage of the Corinthians for his own welfare [2 Cor 12:18]. Titus willingly returned to Corinth with what we know as 2 Corinthians to complete the task of raising the love offering. [2 Cor 8:16-17]

During the period of time between Paul's first incarceration in Rome [A.D. 60-62] and his second incarceration in Rome [A.D. 65], Paul evidently traveled in various places ministering. He had left Titus in Crete to oversee the churches on that island. [Titus 1:5] Sometime during that period Paul wrote Titus this letter, sending Artemis or Tychicus to replace him. He asked Titus to meet him in Nicopolis, the seaport of Philippi. [Titus 3:12]

During Paul second incarceration Titus went to the Roman province of Dalmatia, on the east coast of the Adriatic Sea which separates Greece peninsula from the Italian peninsula. [2Timothy 4:10]

We know nothing more about Titus's life story from the Bible though church tradition says he served as bishop of the Cretan churches for a long time.

Outline

Salutation 1:1-4

1. Sound teaching about church leaders. 1:5-16

    1) Requirements for elders. 5-9

    2) Reasons for qualified elders. 10-16

2. Sound teaching about community life. 2:1-14

    1) Concerning various household groups. 2-10

2) Concerning the fundamental principles of godly living. 11-14

3. Sound teaching about living in this world. 2:15-3:11

   1) Basic commands. 2:15-3:2

   2) Rationale for these commands. 3:3-7

   3) Contrasting manners of life. 8-11

Conclusion 3:12-15

Characteristics and Points of Interest.

1. The tone of the book is fatherly

2. Key words in the book include: sound doctrine [1:9, 2:1, 7-10], good deeds [1:16; 2:7, 14, 3:14], and godliness [1:1, 2:12]

3. The false teachers. The identity of these false teachers is not totally clear. The following can be supported:

1) They came from within the Cretan church. [1:12-13]

2) They belonged to a circumcision group. [1:10]

3) Their teaching was in error.

(1) They held to extra-biblical teaching, built

on Jewish myths and interpretations of the

Old Testament law. [3:9]

(2) They encouraged asceticism. [1:14-15]

They probably taught that the material world is evil, thus the believer should abstain from marriage/sex and eating certain foods.

(3) Their teaching seems to include a certain

affinity to proto-gnostic religious

philosophy mixed with elements of Judaism.

(4) These teachings were false. [1:12]

4) Their motivation was mercenary (to profit financially from their teaching)

5) Their impact was devastating. They disrupted the fellowship doctrinally and morally, devastating whole families.

6) They were not true believers. [1:16]

4. Evidently in Paul's day the Island of Crete was a rather rough undisciplined place. The people had reputation for having little respect for authority, honesty or morality.

5. Titus contains key verses about salvation by grace. [2:11-14, 3:5]

Major Applications

1.The relationship between grace and works - good works are expected but not automatic.

2. The need to live a godly life of good works.

3. How to help a young person getting started in serving the Lord.

Recommended Resources

J.N.D. Kelly, The Pastoral Epistles: I & II Timothhy, Titus, A & C Black, 1963

George W. Knight II, The Faithful Sayings in the Pastoral Letters, Baker, 1979

*George W. Knight III, Commentary on The Pastoral Epistles, [NICGT], Eerdmans, 1992

Abraham Kuruvilla, 1 & 2 Timothy and Titus: A Theological Commentary for Preachers, Cascade, 2021

John F. MacArthur, 1 Timothy: Encouragement for Church Leaders, Moody, 2016

John Stott, Guard the Gospel: The Message of 2 Timothy, IVP, 2021

Warren Wiersbe, Be Faithful, Victor Books, 2009

Philip H. Towner, <u>The Letters to Timothy, Titus</u> [NICNT] Eerdmans, 2006

David C. Verner, <u>The Household of God: The Social World of the Pastoral Epistles</u>, Scholars Press, 1983

A SNAPSHOT OF PHILEMON

Author

 The Apostle Paul. [1:1 ,9, 19]

Date and Place of Writing

From prison in Rome between AD 60-62. Philemon was written at the same time as Ephesians and Colossians.

Recipients

Philemon, Apphia, Archippus, and the church in Colossae. That it was mainly for Philemon is seen in that the personal pronouns [you/your] are singular.

Purpose

1. The primary purpose of this letter was to urge Philemon to receive Onesimus as a Christian brother and not as a thieving slave. [17]
2. Paul also wished to let Philemon know that he hoped to visit Colossae when he was released from incarceration. [22]

Theme

Acceptance of one another in Christian love.

The Story

Philemon was one of the leaders of the Colossian church [v.7]. Along with his wife Apphia, and his son (?) Archippus [Colossians 4:17], Philemon hosted the church of Colossae in his home. [2] The Colossian church seems to have been by-product of Paul's ministry in Ephesus [Acts 19:10]

Epaphras, who was from Colossae may have brought the gospel to them [Colossians 4:12-13]. Philemon, in some way, owed his life to Paul. [v.19]. Philemon had a slave named Onesimus who had run away. Onesimus ended up in Rome. There he met Paul and was saved. Paul was sending him back to Philemon with Tychicus who was bringing this letter and Paul's letter to the Colossian Church with him. [Colossians 4:7-9]

Outline

1. Greetings 1-3
2. Paul's prayer for Philemon 4-7
3. Paul's plea to Philemon 8-21
4. Epilogue 22-25

Characteristics and Points of Interest

1. Paul's letter is warm, gentle, and polite.
2. Some criticize Paul for not condemning slavery in his epistles. Here we see the heart of Paul in this matter in verses 16-17. The church was not in the

business of overturning social institutions, but the influence of Christianity led to the absolution of slavery in much of the civilized world.

Major Applications

1. To teach believers how to relate to one another.

2. How to make an appeal to fellow believers.

3. How to restore broken relationships.

4. To encourage us to learn how Christian leaders can effectively influence others.

5. To show how Christ changes a man.

Recommended Resources

F.F. Bruce, The Epistles to the Colossians, to Philemon and to the Ephesians,
Eerdmans, 2020

William Hendricksen, Philippians, Colossians and Philemon, Baker, 1962

Scott McKnight, The Letter to Philemon, [NICNT] Eerdmans, 2017

*Douglas J. Moo, <u>The Letters to the Colossians and to Philemon</u>, Eerdmans, 2008

H. C. G. Moule, <u>Colossians and Philemon Studies,</u> Pickering & Inglis, 1981

Peter T. O'brien, <u>The Letters to the Colossians and Philemon</u>, Word, 1982

David W. Pao and C. Arnold, <u>Colossians and Philemon</u>, Zondervan, 2012

A SNAPSHOT OF HEBREWS

Author

Unstated in the text. Though historically many have taught that Hebrews was written by the Apostle Paul, most Bible scholars today believe it is best not to attempt to specify the human author.

Recipients

Second generation [2:3] Hebrew Christians living in Palestine but not one specific congregation. [3:1,

12, 6:18, 10:11] A debate centers around whether the warning passages are directed to true believers or to false believers.

Date and Place of Writing

AD 60's probably from Rome. [13:24]

Purpose

To exhort [13:22] and encourage these Jewish believers to go forward in their Christian faith and living to Christian maturity [6:1]. The author attempts to accomplish this purpose by demonstrating that Jesus Christ is superior to the Mosaic System. [3:1, 12:3]

Theme

The Superiority of Jesus Christ and the gospel over the Law of Moses.

The Story

These Jewish believers, under persecution or fearful of it [10:32-34, 12:3-4, 13:3, 13], were tempted to forsake the church and Christian truth and return to the safe haven of Judaism.

Outline

1. The Superiority of Jesus Christ 1:1-10:35

    1) He is Superior to the angels

        (1) Claim 1:1-4 (2) Demonstration 1:5-14

        (3) Application 2:1-18

    2) He is Superior to Moses 3:1-4:16

        (1) Claim 3:1-2 (2) Demonstration 33-6

        (3) Application 3:7-4:16

    3) He is Superior to Aaron 5:1-10:35

        (1) He is Superior as a Priest 5:1-7:28

            a. Claim 5: 1-10. b. Application_5:11-6:20.

            c. Demonstration 7:1-28

        (2) He ministers in a Superior Tabernacle 8:1-5

a. Claim 8:1-2   b. Demonstration 8:3-5

(3) He ministers under a Superior Covenant
8:6-13

(4) He provided a Superior Sacrifice 9:1-
10:35 a. Claim 9:1-12. b. Demonstration
9:13-10:18; c. Application 10:19-35

2. Application: The Believer's Superior Life of
Faith and Endurance. 10:36-13:25

1) Statement of the Proposition 10: 36-39

2) Demonstration of the Life of Faith 11:1-40

3) Demonstration of the Life of Endurance
12:1-

13: 17

3. Conclusions 13:18-25

Characteristics and points of Interest

1. The warning passages [2:1-4, 3:7-4:13, 5:11-
6:12, 10:19-39 and 12:25-29 are central to the
author's purpose. They warn against drifting from

the gospel, spiritual hardness, spiritual apathy, willful sin, and rejection of God's warnings.

2. Hebrews shows the superiority Jesus Christ in his person and death over the Old Testament system of worship. This superiority is used to support the warnings.

3. Commentators are divided over who the warnings were intended for.

1) Some hold that the warnings are intended for true believers and warn believers of the danger of losing their salvation if they abandon the Christian faith and return to Judaism. [Arminian View]

2) Others insist that those warned were false believers who are being warned about the danger of not truly holding to Jesus for salvation.

They were people within the church community who had not yet endorsed Jesus as Savior. [Reformed View]

3) Others suggest that the recipients are true believers, but that the warnings concern what would happen if believers were to do what was

warned against. No true believer would do this. [Hypothetical View]

4) Still others say that true believers are in view, but that the judgment pronounced is not the loss of salvation but chastisement and loss of rewards.

4. Hebrews is full of references to the Old Testament—obviously the intended readers were very familiar with the Old Testament.

5. Jesus is shown to be superior in his person to the angels, to Moses and to the Levitical priests. His sacrifice is superior to that of the Old Testament sacrifices. The New Covenant he established is superior to The Old Covenant of the Law.

Major Applications

1. For those who are questioning the superiority of Christianity.

2. For believers who have stopped growing.

Recommended Resources:

F. F. Bruce, The Epistle to Hebrews, Eerdmans, 2018

Gareth Lee Cockerill, The Epistle to the Hebrews [NICNT], Eerdmans, 2012

*Steven J. Cole, www.Bible.org Lesson 17: When Repentance becomes Impossible. [Takes the Reformed View, but explains all four major views fairly]

M. R. DeHaan, Hebrews, Zondervan , 1959 [This is an older commentary which takes the chastisement/ loss of rewards view]

Paul Ellingworth, The Epistle to the Hebrews, Eerdmans, 1993

William Lane, Call to Commitment: Responding to the Message of Hebrews, Hendrickson, 1995

John MacArthur, Hebrews , 1983 [Reformed View]

Albert Mohler, Daniel L. Akin, et al, Exalting Jesus in Hebrews, Holman, 2017

Peter T. O'brien, The Letter to the Hebrews Eerdmans, 2010

A SNAPSHOT OF JAMES

Author

James, the half-brother of our Lord according to ancient church tradition.

The possibilities include: (1) James, son of Zebedee and brother of John and one of the Apostles, who died very early A.D. 44 [Acts 12: 1-2], (2) James, son of Alphaeus, one of the Apostles, (3) James, the father of Judas the Apostle [Luke 6:16] or (4) James the half-brother of Jesus. [Mark 6:3]

Evidence supporting the early church tradition include facts that he saw the risen Christ and became a disciple. [1 Corinthians 15:7, Acts 1:14] He then became a leader of the Jewish Church in Jerusalem. [Galatians 2:9, Acts 12:17, 21:18-19 and Acts 15]

Recipients

Jewish Christians of the dispersion [not living in Palestine] [James 1:1]. That they were Jewish in seen in 1:1 and in the many references to the Old Testament in the book [e.g., 2:21]. That they were believers is seen in James addressing them as brothers [19 times].

Date and Place of writing:

James died AD 62, so it was written before that date. Lack of reference to severe persecution in the church would argue for a date after the death of Herod AD 44 and AD 49

It was probably written in Jerusalem as James' ministry was centered there. [Acts 8:1 15:13, Galatians 1:18-19]. It is probably the earliest of the New Testament Epistles. Less than 20 years after the death and resurrection of Jesus.

Purpose

To encourage these Jewish Christians to respond to their circumstances in such a way so as to endure to maturity.

Theme

The testing of our faith should lead to steadfast endurance and Christian maturity.

The Story

Unspecified other than that these believers were undergoing trials from outside the church and difficulties within the church.

Outline:

[Note the key to understanding the progress of James is found in 1:19, "Be quick to hear, slow to speak, and slow to anger".

1. Prologue: 1:1-27

   1) The theme: trials produce maturity and rewards . 1:1-12

   2) The proper response to trials 1:13-27.

2. Be Quick to Hear: 2:1-26

   1) Impartiality

   2) Faith and works 2:14-26

3. Be Slow to Speak: 3:1-18

   1) The expression of the tongue is wicked 3:1-12

   2) The expression of wisdom is a righteous life. 3:13-18

4. Be Slow to Wrath: 4:1-5:12

   1) Strife is symptoms of personal worldliness. 4:1-10

   2) Worldliness in its social aspects 4:11-12

   3) Worldliness in its economics aspects 4:13-

5:12

(1) Indifference to God 4:13-17

(2) Indifference to others 5:1-6

4) The need for patience 5:7-12

5. Epilogue: on prayer 13-20

Characteristics and Points of Interest

1. James is characterized by Jewish thought patterns and is set in the early Jewish Church.

2. James contains many parallels with the Sermon on the Mount. [at least 18 of these: e.g.,

James1:2 and Matthew 5:10-12, James 4:11, 12 and Matthew 7:1-5, James 1:22 and Matthew 7:24-27

3. The relationship between author and readers

1) He identifies himself as one of them. "my brothers" "Abraham our father"

2) He is an authoritative leader giving commands.

4. James deals more with practical applicational matters than theology.

195

5. This is a circular letter, not addressed to one specific congregation. He doesn't mention any person by name or location.

6. The "rich" in James [2:6-7, 5:1-6] are unbelievers who might come into the assembly, but who oppressed the believers who were, for the most part, poor.

7. The anointing with oil in 5:14 could mean anointing in a medicinal way [take your medicine] or pouring oil on a person in a ceremonial way, symbolic of prayer or the ministry of the Holy Spirit in the life of the sick person. The sickness in view seems to be sickness caused by some sin.

8. The saving of the soul from death in 5:20 probably refers to the physical saving of a person from physical death rather than in a soteriological sense.

Major Applications

1. James is addressing believers. It is kind of a Christian maturity manual.

2. Warren Wiersbe in <u>Be Mature</u> catalogs the major issues addressed as being patience, practicing the truth, power over the tongue, being a peacemaker and being prayerful.

3. James 2:14-26 has been misinterpreted as teaching that salvation is a product of both faith and good works. It is better to understand James as saying that genuine faith will be accompanied by good works.

Recommended Resources:

Craig L. Blomberg and Mariam J. Kamell, <u>James</u>, [ECNT] Zondervan, 2008

Peter Davids, <u>The Epistles of James</u>, [NIGTC] Eerdmans, 1982

Dan G. MaCartney, James, Baker, 2009

Scott McKnight, <u>The Letter of James</u>, [NICNT] Eerdmans, 2011

*Douglas J. Moo, <u>The Letter of James</u>, Eerdmans, 2021

Warren Wiersbe, <u>Be Mature</u>. Moody, 2008

A SNAPSHOT OF 1 PETER

Author

Peter [1:1]   Other evidence: 2 Peter 3:1 and the author's obvious knowledge of Christ' s life and teaching. Silas either wrote the letter for Peter or delivered it to the churches. [5:12]

Recipients

1:1-2 Believers scattered in Asia Minor — Jews and Gentiles. The majority were probably Gentiles [1 Peter 4:3-4, 1:14,18]

Date and Place of Writing

@ AD 64 probably from Rome. [5:13]

Purpose

To encourage and exhort them to stand firm in the faith [5:12]. To show believers how to live out their salvation in a hostile world

Theme

We live out our salvation through suffering for Christ in the hope of glory.

The Story

These believers were undergoing persecution, religious, social, and civil. [2:13-15,

3:16 -17, 4:4, 12-16]

Outline

1. Salvation: Our Destiny 1:1-2:10

2. Subjection: Our Duty 2:11-3:12

3. Suffering: Our Discipline 3:13-5:14 [This outline taken from Dr. Stanley Tousssaint]

Characteristics and Points of Interest

1. 1 Peter is direct and informal. It resembles a sermon.

2. Use of imperatives. There are many commands.

3. There are several Old Testament quotes and allusions. [1:16, 24-25, 2:6,7,8,9,

3:10-12, 20, 4:18, and 5:5]

4. 1 Peter contains several parallels or allusions to the Lord's teachings [Matthew 5:16 in 1 Peter 3:14. Matthew 5:10-12 in 1 Peter 5:2. John 21:15-17 in 1 Peter 5:5. Luke 13:30 in 1 Peter 4:10].

5. Salvation in 1 Peter goes beyond justification. It is the total transforming work of God in our lives purchased at the cross, being presently realized as we respond obediently to God amid suffering and fully received in the future glory.

6. Two predominant themes are the reality of suffering and the return of Jesus.

7. 1 Peter 3:19-20 is a difficult text. Several interpretations have been proposed: (1) Jesus, in spirit, preached to people through the preaching of Noah, people whose spirits are now imprisoned, (2) Between his death and resurrection, Jesus proclaimed his victory over the demonic spirits who had been imprisoned because of their transgression recorded in Genesis 6:1-4, Jude 6.

8. 1 Peter 3:21 does not teach that baptism brings salvation. Baptism is a symbol of salvation. It is not the water that saves but "the appeal to God for a good conscience," which is the appeal of believing faith symbolized by baptism.

Major Applications

1. 1 Peter will encourage believers facing hostility.

2. 1 Peter shows us how to live out salvation in this world.

3. 1 Peter gives hope to those who find living in this world difficult.

Recommended Resources

Peter H.   Davids, The First Epistle of Peter, [NICNT] Eerdmans, 1990

*Wayne A. Grudem, 1 Peter, IVP, 1988

Karen H. Jobes, 1 Peter, Baker, 2005

Thomas Schreiner, 1, 2 Peter, Jude, Holman, 2003

Edward Gordon Selwyn, The First Epistle of St. Peter, McMillan, 1947

A Snapshot of 2 Peter

Author

Peter the Apostle [2 Peter 1:1, 3:1]

Recipients

Believers scattered in Asia Minor He is writing to the same people he wrote to in 1 Peter. [1 Peter 1:1, 2 Peter 3:1]

Date and Place of Writing

AD.67-68. Probably from Rome [1 Peter 5:13]

Purpose

To stir his readers up to continue to cultivate Christian character. [1:5-13, 3:11]

To warn of false teachers. [2:1-22]

To remind them of the predictions concerning conditions and events associated with the return of Christ. [3:1-13]

Theme

The promises of God motivate us to develop character and be faithful in difficult times.

The Story

A final reminder before his martyrdom. Peter felt it was coming soon [1:13-15]

Outline

1. Prologue: Cultivating Christian character 1:3-15

    1) God's provision for developing Christian character. [3-4]

    2) The process of developing Christian character.

    [5-7]

    3) The rewards of developing Christian character. [8-11]

    (1) Christian character is fruitful. [8-9]

    (2) Christian character brings assurance. [10]

(3) Christian character will be rewarded [11]

4) The urgency of Peter's exhortations. [12-15]

2. The prophecy of Christ's 2nd coming 1:16-3:13

The opportunity for Peter to remind them of these truths is about to end with his soon approaching death

1) The reliability of the prophetic word. [1:16-21]

(1) Jesus' transfiguration confirmed his words [16-18]

(2) Divinely-given prophecy confirms his return. [19-21]

2) A Warning about false teachers   [2:1-22]

3) Assurance of Jesus' return and the events associated with it. [3:1-13:13]

(1) A call to remember the promise. [1-10]

(2) Implications of the promise [11-13]

3. Epilogue 3:14-18

Characteristics and Points of Interests

1. 2 Peter has a unique vocabulary. There are 54 words not used anywhere else in the New Testament.

2. There is a striking similarly between 2 Peter 2 and the book of Jude.

Some explanations of this similarity include: (1) Peter had access to Jude when he wrote, (2) Jude had access to 2 Peter when he wrote, (3) Peter and Jude had access to a third unknown manuscript and (4) Peter and Jude wrote independently of each other. God just inspired them to use the same language.

3. 2 Peter 1:20-21 are key verses explaining the process of the divine inspiration of Scripture.

4. 2 Peter 3:15-16 gives early evidence that the early church considered the writings of Paul to be inspired Scripture.

5. In 2 Peter, Peter refers to happenings during Jesus' life on earth.

(1) 1:16-18 is Peter's testimony about the transfiguration of Jesus recorded in Matthew 17:1-8, Mark 9:2-8, and Luke 9:28-36.

(2) In 1:14 Peter recalls the words Jesus spoke to him recorded in John 21:18-19.

6. The "morning star" in 1:19 is a reference to Jesus as the glorious revealer of God's truth. See Malachi 4:2, Revelation 2:28, and 22:16. The "day" Peter refers to may be (1) the day one is converted, (2) the day of spiritual insight or (3) the day of Christ's return when believers will be surrounded within and without by his glory when he returns.

7. The word "interpretation" in 1:20 does not mean understanding the meaning as we use the word. A helpful translation would be, "No prophecy is of any private derivation."

8. 2:1 is support for the theological position of unlimited atonement. Jesus's death bought the salvation of even the false teachers.

9. The judgment of angels in 2:4 [also Jude 6] should probably be related to the transgression of the sons of God spoken of in Genesis 6:2 as 1:6-7 speak of events taking place in that same time period. [All views of Genesis 6:2 have problems.] What is clear is that some evil angels are confined whereas many others are not.

10. 2:9 speaks about the present state of the unrighteous who have died.

11. Whether 2:20-22 is talking about the false teachers or those deceived by them, what is clear is that they did not ever truly embrace the truth, though they had come to know about it and had even been influenced by it as Peter points out in his proverb about dogs and pigs.

12. Bible scholars debate whether 3:7, 10 and 12 predict a total annihilation of the present earth and universe or just a purifying and refurbishing of it.

Major Applications

1. To encourage believers living in difficult times to develop Christian character.

2. To warn people about false teachers.

3. To remind believers of the reality that Jesus is coming to bring in eternity. God's prophetic word will be fulfilled.

Recommended Resources

*Peter H. Davids, The Letters of 2 Peter and Jude, Eerdmans, 2006

Gene Green and Robert Yarbrough, Jude and 2 Peter, Baker, 2008

John MacArthur, 2 Peter and Jude, Moody, 2005

Joseph B. Mayor, The Epistles of Jude and 2 Peter, Klock & Klock, 1978 Reprint of original published by Macmillan, 1907

Thomas Schreiner, 1, 2 Peter, Jude, Holman, 2003

Warren Wiersbe, Be Alert, Victor, 2010

A SNAPSHOT OF 1 JOHN

Author

Unstated in the text. But vocabulary and style would lend support that it is the same person as the writer of the fourth Gospel and an eyewitness [1:1] Early church tradition all points to the Apostle John, son of Zebedee.

Recipients

Believers [1 John 5:13, 2: 12-14, 3:2, 2:20, 27] Probably Gentiles. Probably not a single congregation)

Date & Place of Writing

1 John seems to have been written after the Gospel of John [2:7-8] [Compare John 13:24 with 1 John 3:8-15. Compare John 8:41-47 with 1 John 5:9-10. Probably written around AD 90, perhaps from Ephesus or Jerusalem (2:19).

Purpose

Stated in the prologue [1:1-4]: to bring these believers into the same intimate fellowship with the Savior that the apostles experienced. [1 John 5:13]

Some Bible teachers believe the purpose of the book is to show us how we can be sure we are saved. This is based on 1 John 5:13. However, the phrase "these things" as used in 1 John usually refers to the verses in the immediate context [2:1, 2:26, 5:9-13].

Theme

Abiding in Christ: the life of continuing fellowship with the Savior.

The Story

The presence of false teachers who had once been a part of the group occasioned the writing of this letter. [2:19, 4:1-3]

Outline: (This outline is from Zane Clark Hodges)

Prologue 1:1-4

1. Introduction: Basic Principles 1:5-2:11

    1) Principles of Fellowship 1:5-2:2

    2) Principles of Knowing Him 2:3-11

2. Purpose for the writing of this letter. 2:12-27

    1) In light of their spiritual condition 2:12-14

    2) In light of world's allurements 2:15-17

    3) In light of the deceptions of the last hour 2:18-

       23

    4) In light of responsibility to abide 2:24-27

3. Development of the theme 2:28-4:19

    1) The theme Stated: Abiding in him leads to

       boldness 2:28

    2) Discerning the children of God 2:29-3:10a

    3) Discerning love for the brethren 3:10b-23

    4) Discerning the indwelling God 3:24-4:16

    5) Theme realized 4:17-19

4. Conclusion 4:20-5-17

1) Love clarified 4: 20-5:3a

2) Love empowered 5:3b-15

3) Epilogue 5: 18-21

Characteristics & Points of Interest:

1. The tone of 1 John is polemical, argumentative, proving points, blunt, and assuring.

2. Emphases in 1 John include: abiding in Christ, the character of God, the person and work of Christ, love, and confidence.

3. Some key words in 1 John: know, believe, abide, love, and light.

4. 1 John was written in simple Greek.

5. 1 John has only one Old Testament citation: 1 John 3:12

6. One key hermeneutical and theological issue in 1 John is the meaning of abiding. Many traditional evangelicals understand abiding as a condition of fellowship in the life of a believer when the believer is walking closely to Jesus. Reformed interpreters understand abiding in Christ as a synonym for salvation. This is a critical issue for

whether the book is about how believers can remain in fellowship with Jesus or whether it is a book giving tests for the reality of faith. For example: Reformed interpreters understand 1 John 1:9 as a salvation invitation. Whereas others see it as referring to how a believer deals with sin in his life.

7. The false teaching infiltrating the church contained elements of

1) Developing Gnosticism. Gnosticism stressed the need for secret wisdom only belonging to the initiated. It emphasized the intellectual. It had a distorted view of the nature of God.

2) Docetism: Docetism denied the true humanity of Jesus Christ and proclaimed the superiority of the spiritual over the physical.

3) Cerinthianism. Cerinthus taught that Jesus was the human person and Christ the divine person which were united at his baptism. Christ left before the crucifixion.

Perhaps all these ideas included in the many antichrists John mentions. [4:1,2:18]

Major Applications

1. As believers, living in close fellowship with Christ involves:

    1) Regular confession of sin.

    2) Commit to obedience to God's word.

    3) Practical love for each other.

2. The benefits of abiding in Christ include:

    1) Joy

    2) Assurance: a clean conscience 4:19-21

    3) Confidence at His coming 2:28

    4) Met needs 3:17

    5) Answered prayer 3:22

Recommended Resources

Daniel Akin, Exalting Jesus in 1, 2, 3 John, Lexham, 2014

John D. Hannah, 1,2,3 John: Redemption's Certainty, Christian Focus, 2017

Karen H. Jobes and Clinton Arnold, 1, 2, 3 John, Zondervan,2014

Colin G. Kruse, The Letters of John, Eerdmans, 2020

John Macarthur, 1,2, 3 John and Jude, Moody, 2016

I. Howard Marshall, The Epistles of John, [NICNT] Eerdmans, 1978

John R. W. Stott, The Epistles of John, Eerdmans, 1964

Warren W. Wiersbe, Be Real, David C. Cook, 2009

Robert W. Yarbrough, 1, 2, 3 John, Baker, 2008

A SNAPSHOT OF 2 JOHN

Author

"The Elder" This term was used to designate a prominent church leader. Church tradition uniformly says the Apostle John was the author. The similarly in vocabulary and style with 1 John would support this tradition.

Recipients

"The elect lady and her children"

This could refer to a specific individual, a specific church, or the church universal. If it was not written to an individual then one must ask "if the elect lady is a church or the church who are the children and the elect sister?"

Date and Place of Writing

Unknown. Anywhere from the 60's to the 90's.

Theme

The truth and the believer.

Outline

1. Salutation 1-3

2. Practicing the truth 4-6

3. Protecting the truth 7-11

4. Farewell 12-13

The Story

The occasion for writing this letter was to warn the church of the danger of false teachers, especially traveling teachers. [10-11]

Characteristics and Points of Interest:

1. Key words in 2 John are: truth, love, abide, and joy.

2. 2 John has similar themes and expressions to the other writings of John.

 v. 1. know the truth. [John 8:32, 1 John 2:21]

v. 2. truth which abides in a person. [1 John 1:8, 2:4, 3:19]

v. 4. walking in the truth . [3 John 3, 4]

v. 5. old/new commandment. [1 John 2:7,8, 3:11. Jn 13:34, 15:12, 17

v. 6. loving one another. [John 13:34, 35, 15:12, 17, 1 John 3;11, 3:23, 4:7, 4:11,12]

v. 7. deceivers. [1 John 2:26, 3:7]

v. 9. abiding. [John 6:56. 8:31, 15:4-10, 16, 1 John 2:6, 10, 14, 17, 24, 27, 28, 3:6, 9, 17, 24, 4:12, 13, 15, 16, 5:8]

v. 12. full joy. [John 3:29, 15:11, 16:24, 17:13, 1 John 1:4]

3. 2 John 12 and 3 John 13 are nearly identical.

4. 2 and 3 John are the shortest New Testament books.

Major Applications

1. 2 John teaches us the need to be loyal to and obey the truth and love each other.

2. Verses 10-11 instruct us about responding to false teaching. Those who enter the church with teachings contrary to foundational Christian truth are not to be received.

Recommended Resources

Daniel Akin, Exalting Jesus in 1, 2, 3 John, Lexham, 2014

John Hannah, 1,2,3 John, Christian Focus, 2017

Karen Jobes and Clinton Arnold, 1, 2, 3 John, Zondervan, 2014

*John Macarthur, 1,2, 3 John and Jude, Moody, 2016

I. Howard Marshall, The Epistles of John, [NICNT] Eerdmans, 1978

John R. W. Stott, The Epistles of John, Eerdmans, 1964

Warren Wiersbe, Be Real, David C. Cook, 2009

Robert Yarbrough, 1, 2, 3 John, Baker, 2014

A SNAPSHOT OF 3 JOHN

Author

"The Elder"—His name is not given. Early church tradition says the author was John the Apostle. Note: the term Elder applies to his seniority, wisdom, and authority.

Recipients

Gaius, an unknown believer and leader in a local church. Probably a Gentile.

He may have been brought to faith by John as John considers him one of his children. [4]

Date and Place of Writing

Unknown. Between the 60's and 90's

Purpose

1. To recommend Demetrius, a traveling teacher, to Gaius and the church.

2. To commend Gaius and encourage him in this matter of hospitality—supporting those who ministered the truth to the church.

Theme
Walking in the truth.. Walking in the truth here includes the loving support for those who faithfully proclaim it.

The Story
John wrote this letter to Gaius, evidently a respected leader in a church [1-3]. First, he wanted to commend Gaius and the church for their support of traveling believers, perhaps traveling teachers, as he calls them "fellow workers for the truth." [5-8]

However, there is trouble. Diotrephes, a self-willed leader in the church, who resisted the authority of John, rejected the ministries of the traveling preachers who came to share with the Christian assembly and refused to support them or let others of the church do so. [9-10] John had written to the church about this before. John is evidently sending this letter to Gaius with Demetrius, who is perhaps another traveling teacher. [12] This letter is perhaps a response to a report from the traveling teachers [v. 6]

Outline

1. Salutation 1-4

2. John commends Gaius for his hospitality 5-8

3. Diotrephes is condemned. 9-11

4. John recommends Demetrius 12

5. Farewell 13-14

Characteristics and Points of Interest:

1. The tone of 3 John is personal and warm yet firm.

2. The key term of 3 John is truth. [3, 4, 8, 12]

3. Note the contrast with 2 John 10-11. False teachers are not to be supported or shown hospitality, but true ones are.

Major Applications

1. The importance of supporting those who do the work of the ministry.

2. The danger of self-willed leaders who try to control everything.

3. The importance of the truth. We testify to it. Walk in it. Work for it.

4. The necessity of confronting sinful leaders.

Recommended Resources

Daniel Akin, Exalting Jesus in 1, 2, 3 John, Lexham, 2014

John Hannah, 1,2,3 John, Christian Focus, 2017

Karen Jobes and Clinton Srnold, 1, 2, 3 John, Zondervan, 2014

John Macarthur, 1,2, 3 John and Jude, Moody. 2016

I. Howard Marshall, The Epistles of John, [NICNT] Eerdman, 1978s

John R. W. Stott, The Epistles of John, Eerdmans, 1964

Warren Wiersbe, Be Real, David C. Cook, 2019

*Robert Yarbrough, 1, 2, 3 John, Baker, 2008

A SNAPSHOT OF JUDE

Author

Jude is a short version of the name Judas who identifies himself as the author of this letter. This almost certainly refers to Judas, the half-brother of Jesus [Matthew 13:55] who became a believer after the resurrection of Jesus [Acts 1:14] Here he also identifies himself as the brother of James, which most probably refers to the well-known leader of the Jerusalem church who is identified by Paul as the brother of Jesus in Galatians 1:19. Church tradition supports this conclusion.

Recipients

Unstated. The content of the book would strongly suggest Christian Jews of Palestine, people familiar with the Old Testament history and Jewish Apocryphal literature.

This letter may have been a circular letter not one for just a particular assembly.

Date and Place of Writing

Uncertain: probably 60's to 80's. Place of origin unknown.

Purpose

To warn the believers of infiltrating apostate teachers and urge them to stand up for the faith.

Theme

It is necessary to stand up for the faith against false teaching.

The Story

Certain false teachers had come into the church and were teaching doctrinal and moral errors. Jude found it necessary to write and encourage the church to contend for the truth and to warm them against these false teachers.

Outline

1. Salutation 1-2

2. Purpose for writing 3-4

3. Condemnation of the false teachers: They are corrupt sinners headed for judgment. 5-16

   1) Three examples of others who were judged. 5-8

   2) A catalog of their sins. 9-13

   3) Their coming judgment. 14-15

   4) Further catalog of their sins. 16

4. Exhortations to the faithful 17-23

5. Doxology 24-25

Characteristics and Points of Interest

1. The tone of Jude is one of tough love, deep concern, and bluntness.

2. The style of Jude is dynamic, with many illustrations and figures of speech.

3. Jude groups things in triads-groups of three. [the three examples of v. 11]

4. Jude is very Jewish. There are many references to O. T. history and other Jewish literature.

5. Some characteristics of the false teachers include both doctrinal and ethical errors: immorality [4, 15, 16], false teaching about Jesus [4], rejection of apostolic authority [8], dependence on extra-biblical revelation [8], ridicule of spiritual realities

 they don't understand [10], greed [11], rebellion [11, 16], selfishness [12], arrogance [16], favoritism [16], divisiveness [19]

6. Verses 5-6 probably refer to evil angels connected with the rebellion of Genesis 6:1-4.

7. Jude's reference to Michael's dispute with the devil [9] can be traced to the Apocryphal work *The Assumption of Moses*. That Jude utilized this story does not mean that the book was divinely inspired. Jude uses the story as an illustration not necessarily as an authentic historical account.

8. "The way of Cain" [11] was that of disobedience and self-will.

9. Jude and 2 Peter 2 are very similar. Some believe Jude utilized 2 Peter [17-18]; others suggest the reverse. They may have utilized the same source materials. Jude 18 is probably referring to 2 Peter 3:3.

10. In verse 14 Jude quotes from the book of Enoch. This does not imply that he considered it Scripture, though it was a well-respected book among the Jews. If Jude says Enoch said this, then he said it. The Enoch indicated is not the one in the linage of Cain, but that in the line of Abel [Gen 5:18-24, 1 Chronicles 1:1-3]. He is the seventh generation if you count Adam.

Major Applications

1. Jude is a warning about the danger of false teachers and the necessity to stand true to the faith.

2. Jude teaches us to learn from the past.

3. Jude reminds us of the connection between wrong teaching and sinful living.

4. Jude reminds us of the reality of future judgment.

5. Jude reminds us to be vigilant both for ourselves and others.

6. Jude 24-25 are verses of great assurance.

Recommended Resources

Peter H. Davids, The Letters of 2 Peter and Jude, Eerdmans, 2006

*Gene Green and Robert Yarbrough, Jude and 2 Peter, Baker , 2008

John Macarthur, 1,2, 3 John and Jude, Moody, 2005

Joseph B. Mayor, The Epistles of Jude and 2 Peter, Klock & Klock, 1978 Reprint of Original published by Macmillan, 1907

Thomas Schreiner, 1, 2 Peter, Jude, Holman, 2003

Warren Wiersbe, Be Alert, Victor, 2010

A SNAPSHOT OF REVELATION

Author

The Apostle John. [1:1, 4, 9, 22:8] God is the ultimate author. [1:1]

Recipients

Seven churches of Asia Minor. [1:4, 11]

Date and Place of Writing

AD 90 to 100. From the Island of Patmos [1:9]

Purpose

1. To show to the church the divine plan for the end of the age.

2. To encourage the suffering believers and exhort them to be steadfast.

Theme

The unveiling of Jesus Christ as judge and king. [1:1]

The Story

Revelation is a record of a revelation given to John by the risen Christ which John was commanded to communicate to churches suffering persecution. [1:11] John had been exiled to the island of Patmos. [1:9] The book gives specific messages to seven churches in the Roman province of Asia located in what we call Turkey today and features a series of prophetic visions concerning the end of human history.

Outline

Prologue 1:1-8

1. The things you have seen. 1:9-20

2. What is now: the letters to the seven churches 2:1-3:22

3. What will take place later. 4:1-22:5

   1)The divine Judge 4:1-5:14

   2) The seven seal judgments. 6:1-8:1

   3) The seven trumpet judgments. 8:2-11:19

   4) Explanatory re-prophecies 12:1-14:20

      (1) Seven personages 12:1-13:18

      (2) The seven years in consummation. 14:1-20

   5) The seven bowl judgments 15:1-16:21

   6) The Babylon prophecies. 17:1-18:24

   7) Final visions. 19:1-22:5

      (1) The coming of Jesus Christ. 19:1-21

      (2) The 1000-year reign of Christ 20:1-10

      (3) The great white throne judgment 20: 11-15

      (4) Eternity 21:1-22:5

Epilogue 22:6-21

Characteristics and Points of Interest

1. Revelation is filled with high drama and figurative imagery.

2. Revelation has a great deal of dialogue.

3. Revelation is an eye-witness account. John relays what he saw and heard.

4. The development of the book is intimated in 1:19: what you have seen [1], what is now [2 & 3], and what will take place later [4-22]

5. Chapters 6-11 seem to be in parallel with chapters 12-20. Both end with Christ's return and reign. Chapteres12-20 are a re-prophecy of the same time-period as chapters 4-11 focusing of personages.

6. The main schools of the interpretation include:
1) The Preterist View. In this view Revelation is only a historical sketch of first-century conditions in the Roman Empire.
2) The Continuous History View. In the view Revelation is a depiction of church history from

the time of John to the Second Coming of Jesus. The attempt is made to match the letters to the seven churches and the prophecies to periods of church history.

3) The Symbolic View. In this view Revelation symbolically pictures the battle between good and evil in every age. It is not prophetic or depicting future events. Some taking this viewpoint would at least concede that we should interpret Revelation 19 as a literal second coming of Jesus.

4) Futuristic View. In this view the visions of Revelation are prophetic and focus on the last part of world history and predict literal events which will take place at the end of the age.

7. Some have seen the seven letters of chapters 2 & 3 as prophetic history of the Church Age with the church of Laodicea being a false church. It seems better to see these as various kinds of churches in the whole of the Church Age. They were historical churches, but the same

characteristics can be found in churches throughout the age.

8. The promises to the seven churches have been understood either as a promise of rewards given to faithful believers or the blessings of eternal life granted to all believers.

9. The symbols and visions have a literal meaning and should be so interpreted unless there is some key in the text which would suggest that we understand them differently. Thomas says, "The proper procedure is to assume a literal interpretation of each symbolic representation provided to John unless a particular factor in the text indicates it should be interpreted figuratively." [Thomas, Revelation 1-7: An Exegetical Commentary, p. 36.] [For example, the first "beast" of Revelation 13 is identified as human. V. 18.]

10. There is nothing in the text that would suggest that the one-thousand-year reign of Messiah

predicted in Revelation 20 should not be understood literally.

11. The Second Coming of Jesus is the focus of Revelation. [1:4, 7, 2:25, 3:11, 11:15, 19:11-20, 22:7, 20] The comings warned about in 2:5, 16, and 3:3, are comings in judgment related to the present not the future.

12. Bible students debate whether the invitation in 3:20 is a salvation invitation for unbelievers or a fellowship invitation for believers.

13. Bible students debate whether Babylon [14:8, 16:19, 17:5, 18:2, 10, 21] should be understood as a real city [a rebuilt Babylon or Rome] or as symbolically depicting the center of the world system opposed to God religiously [17] and economically [18].

Major Applications

1. Revelation gives us great assurance of God's plan for the future. God will prevail.

2. Revelation exhorts us to be faithful in the presence of false teaching and persecution.

3. Revelation assures the faithful believer that God will reward faithfulness.

4. Revelation is also a warning to unbelievers about the wrath to come.

Recommended Resources

G.K. Beale, The Book of Revelation, Eerdmans, 2015

Buist M. Fanning and Clinton E. Arnold, Revelation, Zondervan, 2020

John Macarthur, Because the Time is Near, Moody, 2007

Robert H. Mounce, The Book of Revelation, [NICNT] Eerdmans, 1997

Grant R. Osborne, Revelation, Baker, 2002

John R. W. Stott, What Christ Thinks of the Church, IVP, 1958

*Robert L. Thomas, <u>Revelation, An Exegetical Commentary</u> Moody Press, 1992.

John F. Walvoord, <u>The Revelation of Jesus Christ: A Commentary</u> Moody, 1969